D0119260

DISCARD

6.2/1.0 pt

HELICOPTERS

Paul Eden

GARETH**STEVENS**
PUBLISHING
A Member of the WRC Media Family of Companies

Please visit our Web site at: www.garethstevens.com
For a free color catalog describing Gareth Stevens Publishing's
list of high-quality books and multimedia programs,
call 1-800-542-2595 (USA) or 1-800-387-3178 (Canada).
Gareth Stevens Publishing's fax: (414) 332-3567.

Library of Congress Cataloging-in-Publication Data

Eden, Paul E.
  Helicopters / by Paul E. Eden.
     p. cm. — (Aircraft of the world)
  Includes bibliographical references and index.
  ISBN-10: ISBN 0-8368-6904-4 — ISBN-13: 978-0-8368-6904-0 (lib. bdg.)
  1. Helicopters—Juvenile literature. I. Title. II. Series.
  TL716.2.E34   2006
  629.133'352—dc22   2006004069

This North American edition first published in 2007 by
Gareth Stevens Publishing
A Member of the WRC Media Family of Companies
330 West Olive Street, Suite 100
Milwaukee, WI 53212 USA

Original edition copyright © 2006 by Amber Books Ltd
Illustrations and photographs copyright ©
International Masters Publishers AB/Aerospace–Art-Tech

Produced by Amber Books Ltd., Bradley's Close,
74–77 White Lion Street, London N1 9PF, U.K.

Project Editor: Michael Spilling
Design: Brian Rust

Gareth Stevens editor: Carol Ryback
Gareth Stevens art direction: Tammy West
Gareth Stevens cover design: Scott M. Krall
Gareth Stevens production: Jessica Morris

Measurements appear in statute miles.

Printed in the United States of America

1 2 3 4 5 6 7 8 9 10 09 08 07 06

Cover and title page: Many cities use McDonnell
Douglas MD 500 model helicopters for news, traffic,
and law enforcement purposes.

Contents

Words that appear in the glossary are printed in **boldface** type the first time they occur in the text.

AS 332/EC 225 Super Puma

- Powerful helicopter with two engines
- Carries twenty-four passengers and three crew members

The Super Puma is a medium-sized helicopter designed to carry as many as twenty-four passengers. It first flew in 1978. Most Super Pumas are used to carry workers between land bases and oil rigs at sea. Some also fly as rescue helicopters,

The Super Puma helicopter is used to reach oil rigs in the North Sea off the coast of Scotland.

perform peace-keeping missions around the world, or transport heads of companies or government officials in their luxury **cabins**.

Which Super Puma?

Eurocopter makes three types of Super Puma. The AS 332L1 is the cheapest, with Turbomeca Makila 1A1 engines. The AS 332L2 has a new type of **main rotor**, Makila 1A2 engines, and a **cockpit** with glass displays instead of dials. The EC 225 uses the latest systems for safe flying. The Super Puma's low noise and **vibration** levels provide a comfortable flight.

The Super Puma was developed from the SA 330 Puma. The AS 332L2 model can lift an **underslung** load of 11,023 pounds (5,000 kilograms).

MULTIPURPOSE PUMAS
The Super Puma can be used for many different types of jobs.

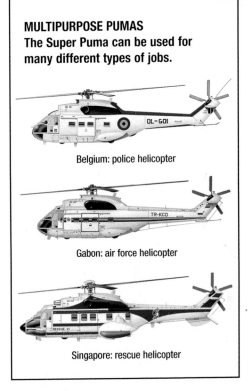

Belgium: police helicopter

Gabon: air force helicopter

Singapore: rescue helicopter

AS 332 SUPER PUMA

Height: 16 ft (5 m)

Special "bags" fill with air in an emergency to help keep the helicopter afloat when landing on water.

The Super Puma carries up to twenty-four passengers.

With luxury seats installed, the Super Puma carries between eight and twelve passengers.

Length: 53 ft (16 m)

AS 350/355

- Reliable, high-performing news helicopter
- Small, powerful helicopter

Eurocopter's AS 350/355 helicopter seats a pilot and six passengers. The AS 350/355 helicopters are reliable, powerful, and economical to operate. In the United States, they are known as the AS 350 AStar and AS 355 TwinStar.

Eurocopter makes a version of the AS 350 specially equipped for news reporting.

Thousands of these helicopters are used throughout the world for news and transportation, for rescue operations, or as emergency medical service (EMS) helicopters.

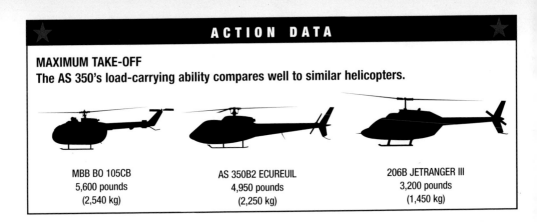

MAXIMUM TAKE-OFF
The AS 350's load-carrying ability compares well to similar helicopters.

MBB BO 105CB	AS 350B2 ECUREUIL	206B JETRANGER III
5,600 pounds	4,950 pounds	3,200 pounds
(2,540 kg)	(2,250 kg)	(1,450 kg)

The AS 350 flew for the first time in 1974.

One or Two Engines?

Special versions of the cheaper, single engine AS 350 serve as rescue helicopters in the mountains and for police work. The AS 350 also takes tourists sightseeing in areas such as the Grand Canyon and Hawaii Volcanoes National Parks. The later model AS 355, with two engines, has more power for lifting heavier loads. It carries a camera and other electronic equipment for live news reports.

In Europe, the AStar is called the *Ecureuil*, which is French for "squirrel." Ecureuils are built in France and Brazil.

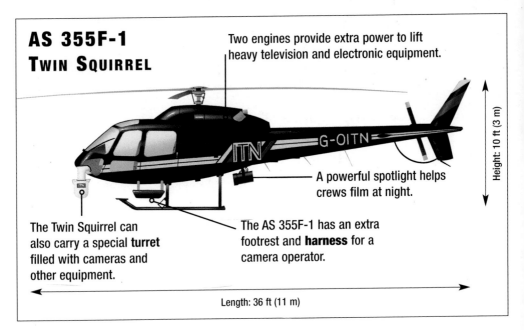

AS 355F-1
TWIN SQUIRREL

Two engines provide extra power to lift heavy television and electronic equipment.

G-OITN

A powerful spotlight helps crews film at night.

Height: 10 ft (3 m)

The Twin Squirrel can also carry a special **turret** filled with cameras and other equipment.

The AS 355F-1 has an extra footrest and **harness** for a camera operator.

Length: 36 ft (11 m)

Aerospatiale HH-65A Dolphin

- U.S. Coast Guard (USCG) rescue helicopter
- Flies from USCG stations and ships along U.S. coastlines and the Great Lakes

When the U.S. Coast Guard wanted a new helicopter to replace its old Sikorsky HH-52 Seaguards, it chose the HH-65A Dolphin.

The Coast Guard received its first Dolphins in 1984. Although the Dolphins were assembled in

Since 1987, the U.S. Coast Guard has used the Dolphin to save hundreds of lives.

France, 70 percent of their parts were made in the United States. The Dolphin flies many missions over large bodies of water, often rescuing people in trouble.

The Coast Guard has nearly one hundred HH-65As based around the United States. All the Dolphins are painted in the USCG's bright white and red colors to make them easy to see in flight over water.

A New Engine

The Dolphin has been safe and reliable. Unfortunately, in hot weather, some of the helicopters used along the coastlines of Florida and Southern California have started to suffer mechanical problems with their engines. The USCG now plans to replace all the older engines in its Dolphins with French Turbomeca Arriel 2C2-CG **turboshaft** engines.

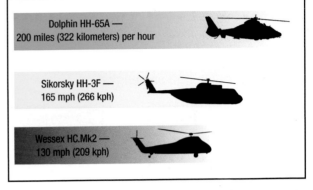

ACTION DATA

MAXIMUM SPEED
The HH-65A Dolphin can travel faster than other rescue helicopters, such as the HH-3F and the Wessex HC.Mk2.

Dolphin HH-65A —
200 miles (322 kilometers) per hour

Sikorsky HH-3F —
165 mph (266 kph)

Wessex HC.Mk2 —
130 mph (209 kph)

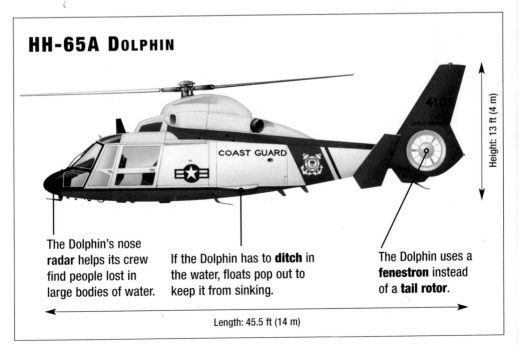

HH-65A DOLPHIN

Height: 13 ft (4 m)

COAST GUARD

The Dolphin's nose **radar** helps its crew find people lost in large bodies of water.

If the Dolphin has to **ditch** in the water, floats pop out to keep it from sinking.

The Dolphin uses a **fenestron** instead of a **tail rotor**.

Length: 45.5 ft (14 m)

1966

Bell 206B-3 JetRanger III

- Around-the-world flight
- Light helicopter with one engine

Bell's JetRanger, one of the world's most successful helicopters, first flew on January 10, 1966. It has a special main rotor with just two wide blades. It is so reliable that it has been used for record-breaking flights around the world. More

The JetRanger helps reporters capture the news as it happens in Denver, Colorado.

than forty-five hundred **civilian** helicopter customers have bought JetRangers. The latest model is the 206B-3.

RON BOWER'S WORLD TOUR
Ron Bower's world tour covered more than 24,800 miles (38,000 km) and twenty-one capital cities.

NORTH AMERICA

Leaves Fort Worth, Texas, on June 28, 1994.
Lands in Fort Worth on July 22, 1994.

The helicopter used no supporting ground crews.

ATLANTIC OCEAN

EUROPE

ASIA

PACIFIC OCEAN

Ron Bower — Globe Trotter

In June 1994, Ron Bower left Fort Worth, Texas, to fly his JetRanger III around the world. After twenty-four days, thirty-six minutes, and twenty-four seconds, he returned to Texas. He flew in stages, landing to refuel between "hops." Bower completed the journey without any problems.

Australian Dick Smith was the very first to fly around the world in a JetRanger III, in 1983. The flight took 260 flying hours, spread over eleven months.

In 1997, British pilots Mike Smith and Steve Good took the record from Bower. They flew around the world in an McDD Model 500D in thirteen days.

206B JETRANGER — DICK SMITH

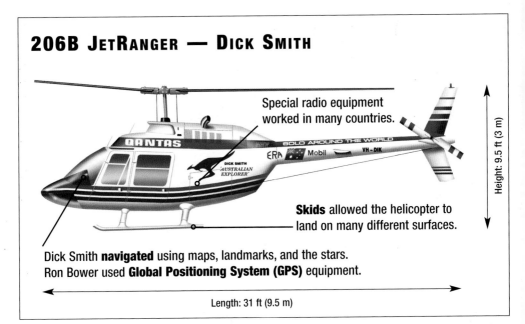

Special radio equipment worked in many countries.

Skids allowed the helicopter to land on many different surfaces.

Height: 9.5 ft (3 m)

Dick Smith **navigated** using maps, landmarks, and the stars.
Ron Bower used **Global Positioning System (GPS)** equipment.

Length: 31 ft (9.5 m)

1976

Bell 222UT

- **Utility** helicopter
- **Popular Emergency Medical Services (EMS) helicopter**

With its **retractable undercarriage** and two engines, the Bell 222 is a sleek, fast helicopter. It is a good helicopter for private service, such as carrying businesspeople to meetings. Bell built a **utility** version of the helicopter called the

Emergency medical services often use Bell Model 222 helicopters.

Model 222UT, with a skid undercarriage. The Model 222 was the first two-engined civilian helicopter ever used in the United States.

12

Emergency Medical Service

Many EMS operators bought Bell 222UTs with special equipment, including **gurneys** and medical equipment to treat patients during flights. Other Model 222UTs flew as passenger transports or to support oil and gas rigs.

Bell stopped building Model 222s in 1989, when it developed the similar Model 230. Today, Bell builds the Model 430, which has a main rotor with four blades. It is based on the original Model 222 design. The Model 222 first flew on

August 13, 1976. The "Airwolf" helicopter from the 1980s TV series of the same name was based on a Model 222.

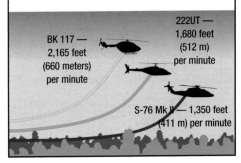

ACTION DATA

RATE OF CLIMB
The 222UT can climb faster from takeoff than the S-76 Mk II but not as fast as the European BK 117.

222UT —
1,680 feet
(512 m)
per minute

BK 117 —
2,165 feet
(660 meters)
per minute

S-76 Mk II — 1,350 feet
(411 m) per minute

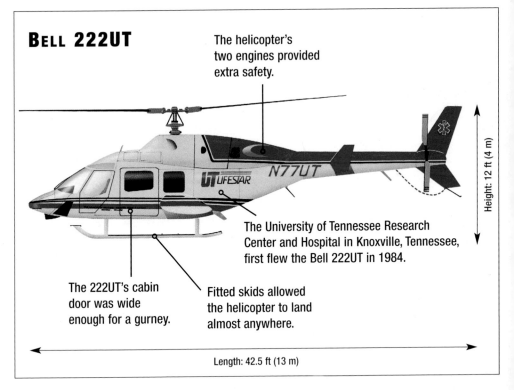

BELL 222UT

The helicopter's two engines provided extra safety.

N77UT

UT LIFESTAR

Height: 12 ft (4 m)

The University of Tennessee Research Center and Hospital in Knoxville, Tennessee, first flew the Bell 222UT in 1984.

The 222UT's cabin door was wide enough for a gurney.

Fitted skids allowed the helicopter to land almost anywhere.

Length: 42.5 ft (13 m)

1980

Boeing Vertol 234 Chinook

- Large helicopter with two main rotors
- Used for heavy-lift operations

The Chinook is one of the most familiar helicopters in the world. The Model 234 Commercial Chinook first flew on August 19, 1980. It has two powerful engines and two large main rotors above its **fuselage**. Boeing built the Commercial

The Commercial Chinook was designed to transport oil rig workers out to sea.

Chinook to transport workers to and from oil rigs in the oceans. Today, all Commercial Chinooks still flying are used as **heavy-lift** crane helicopters.

Four Designs

There were four different types of Commercial Chinook. The 234LR Long Range could carry forty-four passengers. With extra fuel tanks, the 234ER Extended Range could fly 930 miles (1,500 km) farther. British Airways bought six 234ER models. The 234UT Utility was specially designed to work as a flying crane. The fourth model was the 234MLR Multipurpose Long Range, which was like a 234LR, but with a utility cabin.

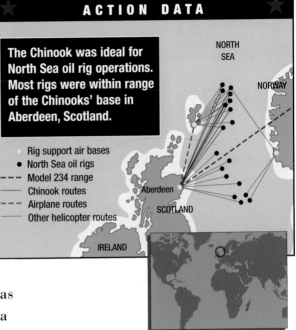

ACTION DATA

The Chinook was ideal for North Sea oil rig operations. Most rigs were within range of the Chinooks' base in Aberdeen, Scotland.

NORTH SEA

NORWAY

• Rig support air bases
• North Sea oil rigs
--- Model 234 range
— Chinook routes
--- Airplane routes
— Other helicopter routes

Aberdeen

SCOTLAND

IRELAND

Today, Chinooks are often used in the logging and construction industries.

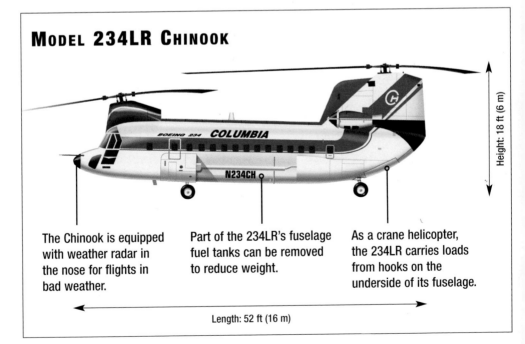

MODEL 234LR CHINOOK

BOEING 234 COLUMBIA

N234CH

Height: 18 ft (6 m)

The Chinook is equipped with weather radar in the nose for flights in bad weather.

Part of the 234LR's fuselage fuel tanks can be removed to reduce weight.

As a crane helicopter, the 234LR carries loads from hooks on the underside of its fuselage.

Length: 52 ft (16 m)

Kaman K-MAX

- Special flying crane helicopter
- New firefighting version — the FIREMAX

The Kaman Corporation of Bloomfield, Connecticut, designed the K-MAX crane helicopter for use in U.S. logging and construction industries. K-MAX helicopters first flew in 1991.

The K-MAX has since been used in Canada, Europe, and Asia. It has **intermeshing rotors**, which means it does not need a tail rotor.

The Japanese use this K-MAX for firefighting and emergency rescue.

The K-MAX also has a very narrow fuselage. All of these features are good for flying into tight — and sometimes dangerous — spaces.

The K-MAX's lightweight fuselage helps focus the helicopter's power on lifting heavy objects.

LOGGING BY K-MAX

Two logging-industry pilots ran a five-day test on the K-MAX in Virginia in March 1994. They carried thirty 6,000-pound (2,240-kilogram) loads of logs a distance of more than 1,900 feet (580 meters) while flying over mountainous terrain in wintry conditions.

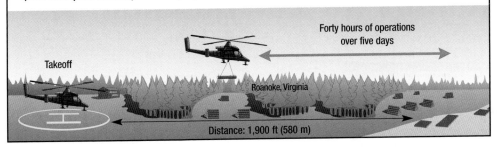

Forty hours of operations over five days

Takeoff

Roanoke, Virginia

Distance: 1,900 ft (580 m)

A Crane and a Firefighter

The K-MAX was the first helicopter in the world designed as a civilian flying crane. It carries all of its loads underslung and needs only a pilot as a crew.

Kaman stopped building the K-MAX in 2004 but has now developed a new version. This model is called the FIREMAX. This firefighting helicopter can carry a large fixed tank that can hold 700 gallons (2,650 liters) of liquid for dropping over a forest fire.

Kaman plans to build other K-MAX models as well as the FIREMAX.

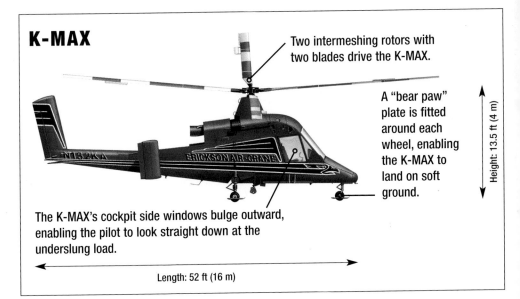

K-MAX

Two intermeshing rotors with two blades drive the K-MAX.

A "bear paw" plate is fitted around each wheel, enabling the K-MAX to land on soft ground.

Height: 13.5 ft (4 m)

The K-MAX's cockpit side windows bulge outward, enabling the pilot to look straight down at the underslung load.

Length: 52 ft (16 m)

17

1965

Kamov Ka-26 "Hoodlum-A"

- Soviet utility helicopter
- Unusual twin-rotor system

The he Soviet-designed Ka-26 light helicopter first flew in 1965. Eight hundred and fifty were built. Fifteen other countries bought the Ka-26. It can be outfitted with different equipment to perform various tasks, such as spraying crops,

The Ka-26 can carry up to seven passengers or 1,550 pounds (700 kg) of chemicals.

transporting passengers, or rescuing people. The helicopter has a wide tail at the end of two long, thin **booms.**

Pods and Tanks

For crop spraying, the Ka-26 carries a large tank and **spray bars**. These hang below the fuselage between the main undercarriage legs. When fitted for passengers, the Ka-26 carries a pod containing as many as six seats instead of the large spray tank.

It also carries a pod fitted with medical equipment when on rescue missions. Another version of the Ka-26 can carry two patients on gurneys, two injured people on seats, and an emergency medical specialist.

The newer Ka-226 is now being built. It is based on the Ka-26, but with two Rolls-Royce turboshaft engines instead.

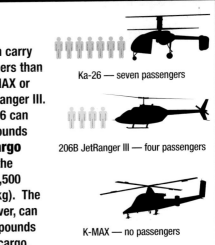

ACTION DATA

MAXIMUM PASSENGERS
The Ka-26 can carry more passengers than either the K-MAX or the 206B JetRanger III. Also, the Ka-26 can carry 1,990 pounds (900 kg) of **cargo** compared to the JetRanger's 1,500 pounds (680 kg). The K-MAX, however, can handle 5,400 pounds (2,450 kg) of cargo.

Ka-26 — seven passengers

206B JetRanger III — four passengers

K-MAX — no passengers

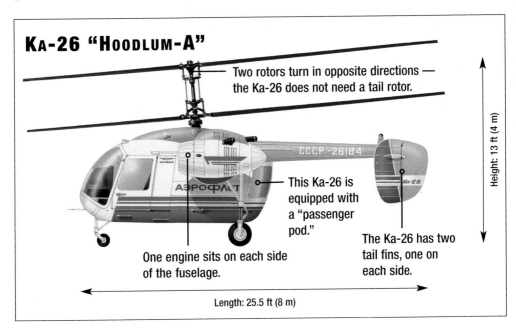

KA-26 "HOODLUM-A"

Two rotors turn in opposite directions — the Ka-26 does not need a tail rotor.

CCCP-26184

АЭРОФЛОТ

This Ka-26 is equipped with a "passenger pod."

The Ka-26 has two tail fins, one on each side.

One engine sits on each side of the fuselage.

Height: 13 ft (4 m)

Length: 25.5 ft (8 m)

1967

MBB BO 105

- Light helicopter
- Can serve as medical emergency vehicle

Messerschmitt-Bolköw-Blohm designed the MBB BO 105. It first flew in 1967 and was later built by Eurocopter. In all, 678 MBB BO 105s were used. This model was usually built in Europe and flown in countries around the world.

The MBB BO 105 is an important tool for ambulance and rescue work.

The last one was completed in 1999. A special main rotor allows the MBB BO 105 to fly in difficult weather conditions. The helicopter normally carries up to six people.

Some MBB BO 105s were sent to Indonesia and Spain.

EMS Helicopter

Its "clamshell" rear door — so called because it opens like the shell of a clam — makes the MBB BO 105 model ideal for transporting the sick and injured. Patients are moved directly from their gurneys into the cabin through the rear door. The MBB BO 105 can fly into small landing zones, making it a fast and efficient way to transport patients to hospitals. It flys at faster speeds than an ambulance can drive. Although it is no longer built, the MBB BO 105 is still used by EMS personnel in the United States, the United Kingdom, and elsewhere.

ACTION DATA

MAXIMUM POWER
The MBB BO 105CB, the AS 355 Ecureuil 2, and the A 109K2 are all used as mountain-rescue helicopters in Europe. The MBB BO 105CB has greater power than the Ecureuil but less than the Augusta A 109K2. All three have twin engines.

MBB BO105CB —
840 horsepower
(626 kilowatt)

AS 355 Ecureuil 2 —
810 hp (604 kW)

Agusta A 109K2 —
1,260 hp (940 kW)

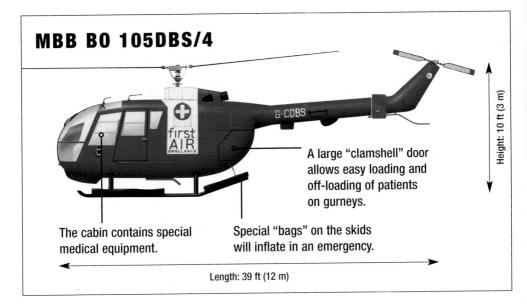

MBB BO 105DBS/4

G-CDBS

first AIR AMBULANCE

A large "clamshell" door allows easy loading and off-loading of patients on gurneys.

The cabin contains special medical equipment.

Special "bags" on the skids will inflate in an emergency.

Height: 10 ft (3 m)

Length: 39 ft (12 m)

1967

McDonnell Douglas MD 500

- Light utility helicopter
- Based on Hughes Model 500

In 1967, Hughes Helicopters, Inc., flew its Model 500 for the first time. In 1984, when the McDonnell Douglas Corporation bought Hughes, it was renamed the McDonnell Douglas MD 500. McDonnell Douglas sold its helicopter line to MD Helicopters

The MD 500E model can be equipped with police searchlights.

in 1999. The MD 500 was so successful that 1,456 of them were built. The MD 500 is popular with pilots and operators because it is economical and easy to fly.

MD 500 Models

The MD 500C model appeared in 1968 and was followed by the MD 500D in 1974. The MD 500D had a more powerful engine, more windows, and an improved tail shape.

The latest model, the MD 500E, was introduced in 1982. Although similar to the MD 500D, it fuselage is pointed in front, and it has a larger, more comfortable cabin for its passengers. The MD 500E can also be fitted with a more powerful engine. The MD 500E carries six passengers and is used by law enforcement agencies. It can also be used as an EMS helicopter to carry two patients. The five-hundredth MD 500E was built in April 1992.

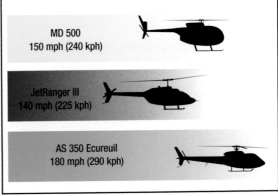

ACTION DATA

MAXIMUM SPEED
The MD 500 has always been faster than its rivals, such as the JetRanger III. It is not, however, as fast as the AS 350 Ecureuil.

MD 500
150 mph (240 kph)

JetRanger III
140 mph (225 kph)

AS 350 Ecureuil
180 mph (290 kph)

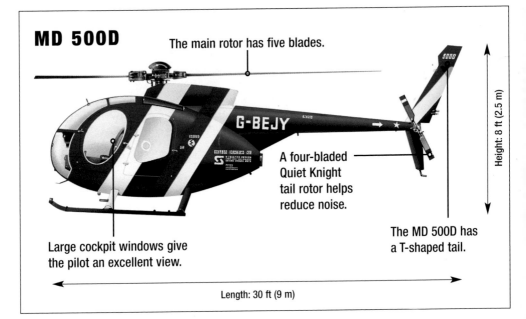

MD 500D

The main rotor has five blades.

G-BEJY

A four-bladed Quiet Knight tail rotor helps reduce noise.

Large cockpit windows give the pilot an excellent view.

The MD 500D has a T-shaped tail.

Height: 8 ft (2.5 m)

Length: 30 ft (9 m)

MD Explorer

- Twin and single-engined light utility helicopters
- NOTAR — NO TAil Rotor technology

Hughes began work on new helicopter technology in 1981. The company wanted to build a helicopter without a tail rotor and with only one main rotor. The NOTAR technology that Hughes developed uses air from the engine that gets

The MD Explorer has a large cabin and no tail rotor.

blown through slots in the helicopter's tail. Most helicopters have the risk of hitting something with their tail rotor — a common cause of accidents. The NOTAR

HOW NOTAR WORKS
NOTAR is a very complex system that takes air from outside and filters it through a fan to create airflow around the tail of the helicopter. This in turn causes the tail to "lift" and enables the pilot to control the direction of the helicopter.

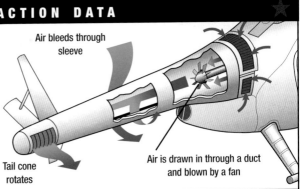

Air bleeds through sleeve

Tail cone rotates

Air is drawn in through a duct and blown by a fan

helicopter has no rotor, so it is much safer to fly. NOTAR helicopters are also very quiet.

MD 520N and MD Explorer

McDonnell Douglas delivered the first NOTAR helicopter — an MD 520N — in 1991. The MD 520N is based on the MD 500E, but with NOTAR technology. McDonnell Douglas also developed the larger MD Explorer. The Explorer has two Pratt & Whitney engines and a large cabin for eight passengers. The MD Explorer is also a popular EMS and police helicopter.

McDonnell Douglas also builds the MD 600N NOTAR helicopter. It carries seven passengers and has just one engine.

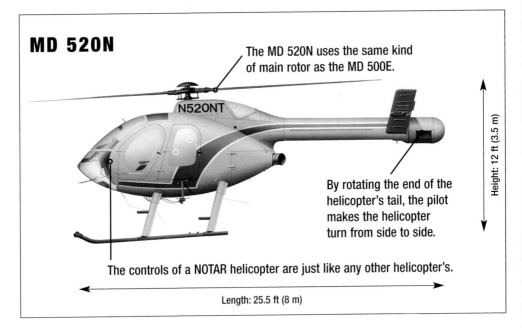

MD 520N

The MD 520N uses the same kind of main rotor as the MD 500E.

N520NT

By rotating the end of the helicopter's tail, the pilot makes the helicopter turn from side to side.

Height: 12 ft (3.5 m)

The controls of a NOTAR helicopter are just like any other helicopter's.

Length: 25.5 ft (8 m)

Mil Mi-26 "Halo"

- Largest helicopter in the world
- Main rotor has eight blades

When Mil began work on the Mi-26 in the 1970s, it wanted to build a helicopter that could lift twice as much as any other helicopter. The Mi-26 has a huge fuselage — the same size as that of a C-130 Hercules transport airplane.

The Mi-26 has a huge main rotor and a giant fuselage.

It can carry one hundred passengers. The two engines of the Mi-26 have twice as much power as the three engines of the huge CH-53E Sea Stallion.

Mi-26 Models

There are many different types of the Mi-26. As well as carrying passengers, the helicopter can also carry cargo inside its cabin — as much as 22 tons (20 tonnes). The Mi-26 has large windows and TV cameras that proved a good all-round view. This model can also be used as a flying crane, a hospital, a firefighting helicopter, and a fuel tanker.

The Russian government uses the Mi-26 to deal with natural disasters such as earthquakes and emergencies such as the 1986 disaster at the Chernobyl nuclear reactor in Ukraine.

The Mi-26 is also important to the Russian oil and gas industries in Siberia, where it is used to carry workers and equipment to remote stations.

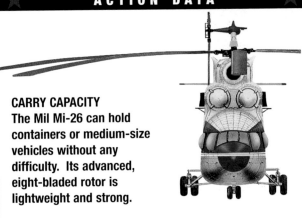

ACTION DATA

CARRY CAPACITY
The Mil Mi-26 can hold containers or medium-size vehicles without any difficulty. Its advanced, eight-bladed rotor is lightweight and strong.

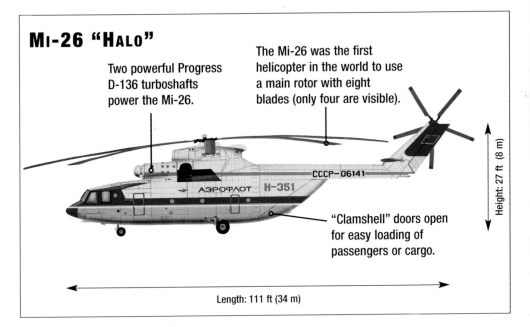

MI-26 "HALO"

Two powerful Progress D-136 turboshafts power the Mi-26.

The Mi-26 was the first helicopter in the world to use a main rotor with eight blades (only four are visible).

CCCP–06141

АЭРОФЛОТ   H-351

"Clamshell" doors open for easy loading of passengers or cargo.

Height: 27 ft (8 m)

Length: 111 ft (34 m)

Robinson R22

- **Light helicopter**
- **Trainer and personal helicopter**

The Robinson Helicopter company of Torrance, California, has been very successful with its simple R22 "personal" helicopter. Many R22 owners use it just like a car.

All R22s seat two people. This easy-to-fly model is often used as

The R22 helicopter has a tiny fuselage and a simple rotor system.

a flight **trainer**, and thousands of pilots learned how to fly helicopters using the R22. Most people buy ready-built R22s, but others choose to build theirs from a "kit."

R22 Varieties

Many types of R22s are available. As Robinson made improvements on its basic helicopter model, it produced the R22 Alpha, the R22 Beta, and its latest, the R22 Beta II model. Customers can also buy an R22 with floats that enable the helicopter to land on water. The floatable model is known as the Mariner.

Another version for spraying crops — the R22 Agricultural — is also available. The special External Load R22 has a hook for teaching pilots how to carry underslung loads.

The R44 version is larger and seats four riders.

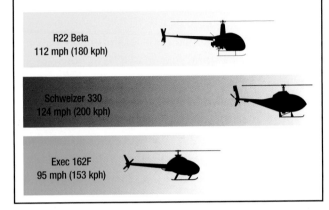

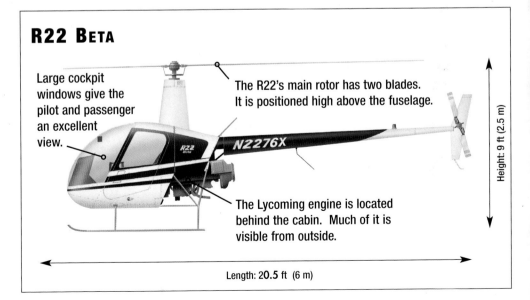

R22 BETA

Large cockpit windows give the pilot and passenger an excellent view.

The R22's main rotor has two blades. It is positioned high above the fuselage.

N2276X

The Lycoming engine is located behind the cabin. Much of it is visible from outside.

Height: 9 ft (2.5 m)

Length: 20.5 ft (6 m)

Glossary

booms — spars or poles that connect the fuselage of an aircraft to the tail

cabins — the inside compartment of aircraft for passengers or cargo

cargo — goods and equipment carried by an aircraft or other transport

civilian — not military

cockpit — compartment where the flight crew controls the aircraft

ditch — to make an emergency landing on water

fenestron — a system that uses a "fan" instead of a tail rotor

fuselage — the main body of a helicopter or airplane

Global Positioning System (GPS) — a navigation system that uses signals from satellites to pinpoint a location on Earth

gurneys — metal tables with wheeled legs used for moving patients

harness — a set of straps used to hold something in place

horsepower — a unit measure for how much power an engine produces. One horsepower is the amount of power produced by one horse per second.

heavy lift — transporting heavy cargo, usually as an underslung load

intermeshing rotors — two main rotors that "cross" each other during flight

kilowatt — a metric unit of power equal to 1.3 horsepower

main rotor — the large rotating blades that make a helicopter fly

navigated — planned and followed a route from one place to another, often using special tools such as a map and compass

radar — equipment that detects out-of-site objects, such as aircraft and ships

retractable — able to fit into the main body of an aircraft during flight

skids — tubes below the helicopter for it to land on

spray bars — long tubes with holes in attached to crop spraying aircraft for spraying chemicals onto crops

tail rotor — the small rotor at the back of a helicopter that keeps it flying in a straight line

trainers — aircraft used for training crew

turboshafts — jet, or turbine, engines that drive a helicopter's rotors

turret — a moveable, bulblike part that sticks out from the main body of a craft or structure and that can hold a camera or serve as a viewing port

undercarriage — the wheels, skids, skis, or floats that hang below a helicopter that are used for landing

underslung — a load hanging underneath a helicopter

utility — designed to perform many different tasks

vibration — movement caused by sounds or other forces

For More Information

Books

Helicopters. Emergency Vehicles (series). Eric Ethan
(Gareth Stevens Publishing)

Helicopters: From Start to Finish. Mindi Rose Englart (Blackbirch Press)

Helicopters. Pull Ahead Books (series). Jeffrey Zuehlke
(Lerner Publishing Group)

Helicopters Stickers. Steven James Petruccio (Dover Publications)

Planes, Gliders, Helicopters: and Other Flying Machines.
How Things Work (series). Terry Jennings (Kingfisher)

Web sites

helis.com — Principles of rotary flight
Explains how helicopter rotars work.
www.helis.com/howflies/prflight.php

American Helicopter Museum
The Web site for the American Helicopter Museum in Philadelphia.
www.gophila.com/C/Countryside/382/Chester_County/242/U/
American_Helicopter_Museum/44.html

U.S. Centennial of Flight Commission — Search and Rescue Helicopters
This celebrates the role of search and rescue helicopters.
www.centennialofflight.gov/essay/Rotary/SAR/HE9.htm

How Stuff Works — How Helicopters Work
Explains how helicopters achieve lift.
www.howstuffworks.com/helicopter.htm

Publisher's note to educators and parents: Our editors have carefully reviewed these Web sites to ensure that they are suitable for children. Many Web sites change frequently, however, and we cannot guarantee that a site's future contents will continue to meet our high standards of quality and educational value. Be advised that children should be closely supervised whenever they access the Internet.

Index

GERMANS

in America

Thomas Schouweiler

Lerner Publications Company • Minneapolis

For Marcella Schouweiler-Stahlmann
and James Thomas Stahlmann,

German Americans who are
also my godparents.

Library of Congress Cataloging-in-Publication Data

Schouweiler, Tom. 1965–
    Germans in America / by Thomas Schouweiler.
        p.   cm. — (In America)
    Includes index.
    ISBN 0-8225-0245-3 (lib. bdg.)
    ISBN 0-8225-1049-9 (pbk.)
    1. German Americans — History — Juvenile literature.
    [1. German Americans — History.]   I. Title.   II. Series:
    In America. (Minneapolis, Minn.)
    E184.G3S353   1994
    973'.0431 — dc20   94-500
                                                        CIP
                                                        AC

Manufactured in the United States of America

1 2 3 4 5 6 – I/MP – 99 98 97 96 95 94

CONTENTS

1
THE HOPE
OF A NEW LAND

In 1990 the U.S. Census Bureau reported that 57,985,595 people in the United States claimed "some measure" of German ancestry. This figure represents 23.3 percent of the population, the largest ethnic group in the United States.

As various immigrant groups—Irish, Jewish, African, and others—have blended into American culture at large, so has American culture absorbed their contributions. Such contributions are especially true of German immigrants, who have an exceptionally long history of immigration to the United States. Germans have been immigrating to the United States for more than 300 years. Many elements of American culture have roots in German society and traditions.

For example, the tradition of spending Sunday relaxing and having fun originated in Germany. The first Europeans to settle in the United States, a strict religious group of English men and women known as Puritans, believed that Sunday should be reserved for quiet religious observance. German settlers shocked the Puritans by enjoying food and drink, as well as keeping their businesses open, on Sunday. This impact can still be seen in all the activities that take place on the second day of the weekend, from professional sports events to backyard barbecues.

Many German foods also are popular across the United States. Bratwurst and liverwurst are German inventions, as are hamburgers, hot dogs, pumpernickel bread, and pretzels. Beer, a German invention, is one of the most popular beverages among adults in the United States. Most American breweries were founded by Germans.

As shown in this lithograph of the 1622 Battle of Hochst, widespread warfare was one reason Germans left their country for a better life in North America.

German people have had an impact on the English language, contributing words such as "kindergarten," "gesundheit," "ouch," and "delicatessen." Germans also introduced Christmas trees to the United States.

One reason that people emigrate from their homeland to a strange and unknown place (as North America was to Europeans in the 17th and 18th centuries) is that conditions at home are difficult. In Germany, war and bad weather sometimes combined to make life so hard that people moved across the ocean in large numbers. Other people left Germany to escape religious persecution: their beliefs so differed from those in power that they were forced to emigrate.

Many left Germany for North America hoping to find land and wealth. One German man wrote to the prince of his region, Nassau-Dillenburg, to explain why he had to emigrate: "I do not know how to make ends meet here anymore. Also the heavy taxation and debts take everything, and my craft is so badly paid that I don't know how to make a single penny. Therefore I won't be able to subsist here much longer."

One German woman, Barbara Ratgeb, sought adventure and wrote that she was "desirous to see more of the world." The first big wave of emigration from Germany, however, resulted from a war that took place in Germany in the 17th century.

The Thirty Years' War

Between 1618 and 1648, when North America had just begun attracting European settlers, a destructive war for land and power was waged among the various rulers of Europe. Much of the fighting took place on German soil. This left the land devastated. Property was burned and looted, crops were destroyed, and disease and starvation ravaged the population. When the war ended with the Treaty of Westphalia in 1648, more than half of the people of Germany had died.

After the war, Germany remained divided into hundreds of individual states, each headed by a king, queen, prince, or duchess. Each ruler felt that it was necessary to build an army out of the already reduced population. To pay for troops and weapons, high taxes were imposed on the people. In some areas 50 to 60 percent of a person's income was taken by the ruler.

As a result of the heavy taxation, Germany entered a severe economic depression. Banks went out of business. Taking advantage of Germany's weak and divided condition, the Dutch and Swedish navies occupied the mouths of Germany's rivers, making foreign trade impossible. None of the individual German armies were strong enough to challenge the invaders.

North Sea

SCHLESWIG-HOLSTEIN

Hamburg

Baltic Sea

MECKLENBURG-WESTERN POMERANIA

BREMEN

Bremen

HAMBURG

LOWER SAXONY

BERLIN

Berlin

NETHERLANDS

POLAND

• Hanover

BRADENBURG

NORTH RHINE-WESTPHALIA

SAXONY-ANHALT

Essen • Dortmund

Düsseldorf

• Leipzig

Dresden

Cologne

HESSE

THURINGIA

SAXONY

Frankfort

RHINELAND-PALATINATE

LUX.

CZECHOSLOVAKIA

SAAR

BAVARIA

FRANCE

• Stuttgart

BADEN-WÜRTEMBERG

• Munich

AUSTRIA

SWITZERLAND

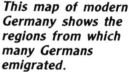

This map of modern Germany shows the regions from which many Germans emigrated.

Germany, once a center of European culture, became a poverty-stricken region. Dissatisfied with their hardscrabble lives, people began to consider leaving Germany for opportunities elsewhere.

Religious Persecution

Changes in the religious culture of Germany also gave some the urge to move from their homeland. The rulers of Germany based their power, in part, on the Protestant faith. Protestantism is a division of Christianity that developed in Germany in the early 16th century and was soon embraced by the German royalty. In turn, the royals demanded that all their subjects also practice Protestantism. During the 16th century, however, another Christian religion developed in Europe. Those who followed this faith were called Anabaptists, meaning re-baptizers. Anabaptists felt that believers in their faith should be old enough to choose membership.

Therefore, they were baptized a second time when they joined the new religion. Anabaptists also believed that the Protestant rulers of Germany cared more for political power than for God.

The rigidly Protestant governments considered the Anabaptists a threat and had been trying to wipe them out for many years. In 1528 Emperor Charles V of Germany decreed that being an Anabaptist was an offense worthy of death. Charles V believed that God, in accordance with Protestant beliefs, divinely decreed that he, Charles V, should rule the land. The emperor did not tolerate his subjects' belief in anything other than the Protestant faith, because they then might question his right to rule Germany. Charles V ordered that Anabaptists be tortured and killed and that their homes be burned to the ground. In some regions of Germany, even a house where an Anabaptist temporarily lived could be seized. Thousands of Anabaptists paid for their faith with their lives. Countless others had to move constantly to elude authorities.

The Anabaptists, however, were not one large group, as the Protestant government saw them. Among the Anabaptists, several different groups of religious dissenters existed. A Frankfurt lawyer named Francis Daniel Pastorius was the leader of one of these religious sects.

Pastorius was born in Sommerhausen, Franconia, in Germany in 1651. Pastorius was a Quaker, one of a sect of Anabaptists that also believed in a simple life and a direct relationship to God. Pastorius wanted to improve the conditions of his fellow Quakers by establishing a colony in North America, where they would have the freedom to worship as they chose. He purchased 15,000 acres of land in what is now Pennsylvania from the English Quaker William Penn, for whom the land is named.

Pastorius learned of the opportunities in North America from Penn. Penn was granted a large tract of land by the British government as a repayment of a family debt. He wanted to use this land as a haven for poor and oppressed people, especially those experiencing

A Quaker meeting in colonial North America. The first group of Germans to settle permanently in the United States was Quaker.

religious persecution in their homelands. During a tour of the German Rhineland, Penn witnessed the devastation of land once rich and productive. He saw that people were plagued by economic depression, crop failure, famine, religious persecution, and high taxes. He spoke to them about how they could escape harsh conditions in Germany for opportunities across the Atlantic.

The combination of poverty and religious intolerance led the first group of German immigrants to set sail with Pastorius in 1683. Thirteen families from Krefeld, a part of Germany near the Dutch border, sailed for North America on the ship *Concord.* To pay for the long, dangerous journey in dirty, crowded immigrant ships, many would-be settlers had signed on as redemptioners. This meant that they agreed to work for a certain number of years as the servants of colonists already settled in North America to pay for their passage.

11

The voyage began on June 10, 1683. The 80 people on board the *Concord* endured stormy weather and several mishaps. During one storm, two carved lions that supported the ship's bell fell onto Pastorius, nearly breaking his back. During another gale, Pastorius took a nasty fall and was confined to his bed for several days. Other passengers suffered illness and injury; a sailor went insane; and the ship was repeatedly attacked by a whale.

Ten weeks after they set sail, Pastorius and his company arrived in Philadelphia. The party moved inland and soon established Germantown, the first German settlement in the North American colonies. Pastorius became the first mayor of Germantown.

The early days of the settlement were full of difficulties. Pastorius shared in the hardships of his comrades. He lived in a wooden shack, 15 by 30 feet, with

These drawings of Germantown, the first German settlement in the North American colonies, were found in a mid-19th-century sketchbook.

oil-soaked paper for windows. Over the door to his humble dwelling, Pastorius hung the motto "Small is my house, it welcomes the good man; let the godless one stay away."

Germantown was a peaceful place. Crime was practically nonexistent. A court met once every six weeks to administer punishment to lawbreakers, but it frequently adjourned because there was no business to take care of. The most common offenses were occasional cases of drunkenness or neglected fences. One of the more amusing crimes recorded was that of a man named Müller, who was jailed for attempting to smoke 100 pipefuls of tobacco in one day to satisfy a bet. Another time, a man named Caspar Karten was put in jail for calling a police officer a "rogue."

Soon, thousands more Germans poured into Pennsylvania. Some, like Pastorius's group, sought religious freedom. Many others had grown tired of trying unsuccessfully to grow crops and eke out a living in a land that was still devastated by the effects of the Thirty Years' War. There were an estimated 45,000 in the colony by 1745. In 1766 Benjamin Franklin reported that Germans made up about one-third of the white population of Pennsylvania. In addition to the Native Americans who were already living in the area, the rest of the population was composed of Swedish, Dutch, English, Welsh, Scottish, and Irish immigrants.

The Pennsylvania Dutch

The Germans who emigrated to Pennsylvania came to be known as the Pennsylvania Dutch. "Dutch" is the word that describes people from Holland, not Germany. The name "Pennsylvania Dutch" evolved when English-speaking colonists confused the word "Deutsch," which means German, with the word "Dutch." The misunderstanding became so widespread that even the German settlers began to refer to themselves as "Dutch."

The Pennsylvania Dutch first settled around Philadelphia and Germantown. Later, they spread into the eastern and southern sections of Pennsylvania and eventually moved into Maryland, Virginia, and the South.

Religious Life

The chief reason that German settlers were attracted to Pennsylvania was the colony's religious tolerance. William Penn intended Pennsylvania to be a place where all people could be free to worship according to their consciences. In most North American colonies religion was established by the local governments, just as it had been in Europe.

The Pennsylvania Dutch were divided into two groups. One was the so-called "church people." These people belonged to one of two large and established Protestant churches—the Lutheran and the Calvinist.

Many German immigrants were farmers.

The other Germans were called "plain people," because of their plain dress and style of worship, or "sectarians" because they belonged to small groups (sects) that emphasized beliefs quite different from each other. They differed over ceremonies, such as baptism, and over interpretation of the Bible. The Mennonites and the Amish—descendants of the Anabaptists—were the largest of the sects. Altogether, there were more than two dozen different sects, including groups named Dunkards, River Brethren, Quietists, the Mountain Men, the New Born, the Inspired, and the Society of the Woman in the Wilderness.

One thing that all sectarians had in common was their emphasis on Pietism—the religion of the heart or conscience. The central idea of Pietism is that each person can communicate directly with God without the help of priests or churches.

Most important to the sectarians was that they wanted nothing to do with politics and government. They simply wanted to worship as they saw fit. They wanted to farm the land, raise their families, and be left alone by governments and official churches. Many were pacifists—they believed it was wrong to fight as a soldier or do violence to another human. These German immigrants not only refused to take part in military affairs, but also rejected participation in the politics and government of their colony.

Another belief held by sectarians was their opposition to slavery. African slaves were common in the colonies. By 1688 Mennonites had announced their anti-slavery feelings to their neighbors around Pennsylvania. One Mennonite man traveled many miles to visit a friend. Arriving at his friend's farm after a long and difficult journey, the Mennonite was shocked to find that the man owned slaves. He was so opposed to the practice that he slept in the woods that night and returned to his home the next day.

The distinctiveness of sectarians exists to this day. Sectarians still dress simply and observe many of the old ways. Many Amish live in Pennsylvania and Iowa, as well as in other states, observing the old ways from

The Pennsylvania Dutch became known for their folk art, such as this "Christian house blessing," a painted wall hanging.

15

colonial times. They wear old-fashioned clothing and worship the same way they did 300 years ago. They shun modern conveniences, refusing to use electricity or cars. They live much as they did in Pastorius's time.

Community Life

For the Pennsylvania Dutch, community life centered on the farm. Early settlers selected wooded areas for their homesteads, which they cleared tree by tree. They built sod shanties at first, then log cabins, and eventually stone farmhouses. The houses were built of fieldstone—stones gathered from the surface of the ground and fitted together.

This Mennonite girl in Lancaster, Pennsylvania, lives much as her immigrant ancestors did almost 300 years ago.

The most impressive building on a typical Pennsylvania Dutch farm was usually the barn. The settlers built large, two-story barns, sometimes more than 100 feet long. They resembled the barns of the Black Forest region of Bavaria in southern Germany. Stone formed the base of each barn, and large timbers formed the roofs. In front, an overhang of five to ten feet, called a "vorschuss," protected cattle or horses from the weather. The farmers painted the arches over the windows and doors white. Traveling barn painters or farmers themselves painted bright, eye-catching circular designs called hex signs between the windows. For some Pennsylvania Dutch, hex signs reflected a belief in elements of the occult—magic and unseen mystical forces. Although they remained deeply religious, superstitious farmers sometimes consulted mystics for astrological predictions about future crops and other matters. For others, the hex signs were merely decorative.

The Pennsylvania Dutch farm was as self-sufficient as possible. Farm families raised a wide variety of crops: corn, oats, rye, barley, flax, and tobacco. Usually, each family had a vegetable garden, an orchard, and beehives. Pigs, ducks, geese, guinea hens, and chickens also provided food. Cows were raised for both dairy and meat. Easily preserved vegetables, such as cab-

bages and turnips, were stored through the cold winters in root cellars. The Pennsylvania Dutch were also probably the first North Americans to raise asparagus and cauliflower.

Modern-day Amish schoolchildren at school in Pennsylvania

The colonial Germans considered education—especially reading and writing—a high priority. Pastorius was the first German teacher in the colonies, working at an English Quaker school in Philadelphia before taking charge of the first German school in Germantown in 1702. Church teachings provided the basis for education. Students paid for their own schooling, and contributions from citizens also helped support the German schools. Teachers in these schools used German exclusively and did not teach English at all.

The Valley of the Mohawk

Another large group of Germans settled in North America in the early 1700s. About 10 miles north of Albany, the present-day capital of New York State, the Mohawk River flows into the Hudson River. Before the Germans arrived there, the region was occupied by a confederacy of six Native American tribes known as the League of the Iroquois. The League consisted of the Mohawk, Cayuga, Seneca, Onondaga, Oneida, and Tuscarora tribes. As the colonies grew, white settlers overran the lands of these tribes, killing members of the tribes.

German settlers came to the New York colony in the early 1700s. They formed the largest single immigrant group in North America before the Revolutionary War (1775–1783). Most came from the Palatinate, a section of southwestern Germany along the Rhine River. During the reign of Queen Anne (1702–1714), the British began to actively promote settlement of New York by Germans. The British needed the Germans for labor to harvest North America's natural resources, such as timber and tobacco.

The Germans recruited by the British immigrated as redemptioners. In return for transportation across the ocean and settlement expenses, the immigrants agreed to work for the British navy until their debt was paid off. This program was so popular among impoverished Germans that the British government soon had more volunteers than work to be done.

The first group came down the Rhine in 1708 under the leadership of Joshua Kocherthal. Their immediate destination was Holland, where they waited for transportation, first to Britain and then to the colonies. By the next year, 4,000 immigrants from the Palatinate were arriving in North America via Holland each month. Their journey took four to six weeks.

In 1709 Joshua Kocherthal's group of refugees founded Neuberg (now Newburgh) on the Hudson River north of New York City. By 1711 the British govern-

The hex sign and low-slung roof of this barn were typical features of German-American farms.

ment had spent more than 100,000 pounds to establish seven villages of German settlers. In the following years, the German immigrants began to move north. By 1713 some 50 families were living in the Schoharie River Valley south of present-day Schenectady, and others had moved into the scenic Mohawk River Valley. For many years, this entire region was known as the "German Flats" and noted as excellent farming country.

The Germans prospered in New York as they did in Pennsylvania. By 1750 they had constructed about 500 houses, mostly of stone, on a 12-mile strip of shore along the Mohawk.

Other Areas of German Settlement

Because they were often opposed to the practice of slavery, German sectarians did not initially settle in the American South—where slaves worked on large plantations—in large numbers. Nor were many comfortable

19

in New England, where the Puritans—the devout settlers from England—did not tolerate religious dissenters. But the Germans did not restrict themselves to Pennsylvania and the Valley of the Mohawk. In Virginia the earliest German settlement was at Germanna in present-day Orange County, where 12 families set up an ironworks in 1741. Soon afterward, 80 German families from the area of Württemberg, Germany, came to Virginia. One town in Virginia, Staufferstadt (later renamed Strasburg), was founded by a man named Jacob Stauffer. Since land grants were based on family size, Stauffer obtained the land in 1728 by claiming every horse and cow he owned as a member of his family.

Typically, German-American towns were very carefully designed. Streets were laid out at right angles in a checkerboard pattern. A church, a school, a storehouse for supplies, and an orphanage were included in the plans for each city.

A German immigrant named Robert Harper established the city of Harpers Ferry in present-day West Virginia. Hundreds of German families poured into the fertile Shenandoah Valley soon afterward. The Germans avoided the tidewater country of colonial Virginia, however, because they objected to the use of slaves already in practice there. By 1775, the year the American Revolution began, Germans had spread throughout the colonies. There were 25,000 Germans in New York, 110,000 in Pennsylvania, 15,000 in New Jersey, 20,500 in Maryland and Delaware combined, 25,000 in Virginia, 8,000 in North Carolina, 15,000 in South Carolina, and 5,000 in Georgia.

Prominent Germans of Colonial America

One German immigrant who made an impact on U.S. history during the colonial period was John Peter Zenger. Zenger was born in Germany in 1697 and came to North America when he was 13 years old. His parents died during the voyage, and Zenger was apprenticed to a printer before even setting foot in the colonies. Through his apprenticeship, he learned the printing business, and in 1726 he set up a printing shop of his own.

In 1733 Zenger was editor and publisher of the *New York Weekly Journal.* He began printing articles that were highly critical of the oppressive policies of the governor of New York, Sir William Cosby. Although Zenger's friends probably wrote the critical articles, Zenger, as publisher of the paper, was legally responsible.

In 1734 Governor Cosby retaliated by having Zenger arrested and held in jail for 10 months. He awaited trial on charges of criminal libel—the crime of printing something defamatory (damaging to the reputation of another person). Zenger's attorney, Andrew Hamilton, argued that the newspaper's criticism of Cosby was not unlawful because the statements were true. Zenger was found not guilty. This verdict became an important precedent in cases involving freedom of the press.

There are many "firsts" among the Germans who came to the United States during its earliest years. In 1690 William Rittinghausen set up the colonies' first paper mill in Germantown. Caspar Wistar founded the glassmaking industry in the United States.

Differences in religious practice and the language barrier may have kept many German immigrants from blending into colonial society. Yet through their industriousness, German Americans were beginning to have an effect on their new country.

Richard Wistar (above) ran the glassworks his father founded in the mid-18th century, producing items such as this sugar bowl.

2
THE REVOLUTION AND AFTER

In the 1770s, the days of British rule over the American colonies were drawing to an end. Britain's desire to govern and tax the colonies clashed with the colonists' growing desire for independence. Hostilities between Britain and the colonies first flared in March 1770. British soldiers, goaded by angry colonists, opened fire on a crowd, killing five and wounding six in what came to be known as the Boston Massacre. War finally broke out in Massachusetts on April 19, 1775, with the battles at Lexington and Concord. Three hundred thousand Germans—10 percent of the entire colonial population—would play an important part in the American Revolution.

Peter Muhlenberg, a Lutheran pastor and the son of German immigrants, removed his robes one Sunday morning in 1776 and said to his congregation, "There is a time for preaching and praying, but also a time for battle."

Soldiers of German descent from all over the rebellious colonies volunteered for the American militia. A company known as the German Fusileers formed in Charleston, South Carolina. In the valley of the Mohawk, German-American soldiers made up four battalions. They were first tested when British forces laid siege to their dilapidated fortress on the Mohawk River. The 750 soldiers inside fought stubbornly and defended their fort.

General Washington, commander of the American troops, trusted the German colonists and selected a number of them to be his bodyguard, a group commanded by Major Barth von Heer.

Peter Muhlenberg, a German-Lutheran pastor, ended his sermon on a Sunday morning in 1776 by saying, "There is a time for preaching and praying, but also a time for battle, and such a time has now arrived." Standing in the pulpit before his congregation, he removed his pastor's robes. Underneath them he was wearing the uniform of a colonel of the Continental army. He later became a general and fought in the battles of Brandywine, Germantown, and Yorktown.

Baron de Kalb, a soldier of fortune (professional soldier) from Bavaria, Germany, came to North America with the Marquis de Lafayette, a French soldier and statesman. He became a sincere patriot and died at the Battle of Camden in South Carolina.

Baron Friedrich Wilhelm von Steuben made one of the greatest military contributions to the American cause. Benjamin Franklin met von Steuben, a former soldier in the Prussian army, in Paris. Franklin was so impressed by this man that he recommended von Steuben to the Continental Congress—the group of colonists that was organizing the rebellion against Britain. Von Steuben arrived in the winter of 1777–78, while General Washington and his troops suffered at Valley Forge. Von Steuben soon joined them. He was such an effective commander that he established a code of discipline that was used throughout the Continental army. After the war, Congress rewarded him for his superior service.

One of the best-known stories of the Revolutionary War concerns the young woman called "Molly Pitcher," who was the hero of the Battle of Monmouth. Born Maria Ludwig, Molly was the daughter of German immigrants and was born near Trenton, New Jersey. Her husband enlisted as a gunner in the First Pennsylvania Artillery and lived at the Valley Forge camp with the rest of Washington's troops.

Like Martha Washington and the wives of many other soldiers, Molly joined the troops in the camp to help the war effort by cooking, washing clothes, and helping wherever she was needed. She was with the army when the Battle of Monmouth was fought on Sunday, June 28, 1778—an extremely hot day. Molly carried pitchers of water to the soldiers to ease their thirst. But her contribution did not end there. During the battle, her husband was wounded. Molly took his place alongside the other soldiers, firing his cannon throughout the rest of the battle.

Patriots, Tories, and Conscientious Objectors

The struggle for independence, which divided the colonists into patriots and loyalists (or Tories, allied with the British monarchy), sharply split the German immigrants. Many of the sectarians were devoted pacifists and refused to partake in military service. Many of these Germans who refused to take up arms served in other ways. Some took care of soldiers in their homes or furnished supplies to General Washington's army. Throughout the terrible winter at Valley Forge, Pennsylvania Germans kept the army from starving by getting supplies to the tired soldiers. Others set up hospitals and served in them. The Moravians—a Protestant sect of German immigrants from Bethlehem, Pennsylvania—tended the forces at Valley Forge. After the Battle of Brandywine, a group of German pacifists set up and staffed a hospital in a nearby schoolhouse.

Maria Ludwig, known as "Molly Pitcher," became famous for her bravery during a battle of the Revolutionary War.

Baron von Steuben drilling the troops at Valley Forge. Because he didn't speak English, other officers translated von Steuben's orders to the troops.

Although in some areas the Germans' refusal to enter military service was respected by their patriotic neighbors, it was not so in all places. Many non-German colonists deeply mistrusted German sectarians who refused to fight. Some Germans were avoided by their peers and in some cases even banished from their communities. Some non-German colonists did not understand that while their German neighbors refused to join them in the fighting, they were happy to feed and protect the Revolutionary armies. This position, shared by Amish, Mennonite, and other German religious sects, was summed up in a declaration issued by the Number of Elders and Teachers of the Society of Mennonites on December 7, 1775:

> We receive with cheerfulness...all men of what station [status] they may be—it being our principle to feed the hungry and give the thirsty drink;...but we find no freedom in giving, or doing, or afflicting in anything by which men's lives are destroyed or hurt. We beg the patience of all those who believe we err in this point.

The Mennonites also suffered some divisions among themselves on the issue of pacifism. Some believed that they were obliged to fight for their new land; others were opposed. Some believed that it was all right to fight against the Native Americans who attacked their outermost settlements in the wilderness, but not to fight in the Revolutionary War.

The German people who belonged to the German Lutheran or German Reformed Churches did not share the sectarians' objections to military service. From these Germans, almost all of them loyal to the Revolutionary government, came some of the great military heroes of the war.

The Hessians

One group of Germans in the Revolutionary War period fought on the British side. These were the paid professional soldiers known as Hessians. Although brought to the colonies to fight, many remained as settlers.

When the war began, the British were faced with a lack of soldiers. They sought aid from the rulers of the small German states in Europe, who were eager to supply soldiers in return for money. Britain paid a total of seven million pounds to Hessians. The troops came from six German states: Brunswick, Hesse-Hanau, Waldeck, Anspack-Bayreuth, Anhalt-Zerbst, and Hesse-Cassel (which is where the name "Hessians" came from). Eventually, more than 30,000 German soldiers were sent to the colonies.

Of these 30,000, about 12,000 stayed to make their homes in the new United States. In fact, many of the Hessians agreed to fight for Britain only to get to North America. A report to England from Hessian headquarters in the colonies stated that "many of them may have been prompted to take the chance of a free passage to this country, and thus in this matter finally get away from Europe, instead of having to work about four years to redeem the cost of their crossing."

Early in the war, the Continental Congress began a campaign to lure the Hessian soldiers away from the British army. The Hessians were promised all the rights of American settlers, plus grants of land ranging from 50 acres for a common soldier to much larger grants for officers.

At least 6,000 Hessians deserted to the side of the Revolutionary army during the war, finding help and shelter with friendly German patriots. Near the end of the war, two states, South Carolina and New Jersey, sent out pamphlets in German urging the Hessians to stay in the United States and take up land. The colonists were anxious to have the Hessians desert the British army in order to improve American chances in the war. A greater number of settlers on American soil would also make it more difficult for British armies to occupy conquered land.

After the war, the Hessians quickly resumed peaceful activities, becoming skilled laborers, farmers, and sometimes teachers. Settled German Americans helped some

In this 1805 drawing of a German-American school, the students' names are listed at the bottom. Education was important to German immigrants.

27

of the Hessian prisoners of war in Pennsylvania and Virginia escape to the west. These soldiers were among the first pioneers to cross the Allegheny Mountains to the expanding frontier.

The Early Years of the Republic

The end of the Revolutionary War came officially with the Treaty of Paris in 1783. By 1790 the Germans in America numbered about 360,000 in a total population of 3,929,214. Many farmed the land. The artisans among them ran businesses and built a reputation as skilled craftspeople and hard workers. These people gave the new nation a stability that was needed during its first difficult years. German language books and newspapers flourished, as did early choral societies, which reflected the German love for music.

Immigrants of the 19th Century

During the last years of the 18th century and the early years of the 19th century, immigration to the United States fell off sharply. The political and military turmoil of the Revolutionary War discouraged would-be immigrants. After the American Revolution, western Europe was beset by the French Revolution.

Brought about by economic difficulties and demands for more democracy in government, the French Revolution began in 1789 and continued off and on for many years. The ideas of the revolution spread across Europe. Peasants were no longer satisfied with the idea of the divine (God-given) right of royalty to rule over them. They came to believe that they had the right to own land, to worship as they pleased, and to create a representative government. These concepts did not take hold in Germany at the same time as they did in France, but when democratic ideas came to Germany in the 19th century, they were surely influenced by the French Revolution.

Because they were fighting wars with France, many German rulers would not let soldiers leave the country. They were needed for German armies. Skilled German artisans were also needed at home. Many German states issued special decrees forbidding them to leave the country. Nevertheless, they did leave. One emigrant, a glassblower from Hanover, had himself smuggled to the United States as a corpse in a coffin.

Many U.S. citizens went to Germany during the early 1800s to recruit workers for jobs available in the United States. Some of the newest states, such as Ohio, followed the example of William Penn and advertised their vast and rich farmlands in German publications. The enticement worked. German immigration began to rise. In 1832 just over 10,000 Germans immigrated to the United States. Five years later, 24,000 people left Germany to settle on the frontier.

Above: A family in Germany reads a letter from an emigrant relative praising the good life in the United States. Left: Germans in Hamburg, Germany, board a steamer ship bound for New York in 1874.

From 1820 to 1900, about 5,000,000 Germans moved to the United States. In fact, during the last half of the 19th century, German immigration exceeded that of any other single country. Throughout the century, German immigrants arrived in ships that landed at every major American port. Although many immigrants remained in the eastern part of the United States, many thousands headed for the Midwest and eventually the West and the Southwest. They also sailed up the Mississippi River from the port city of New Orleans to settle in the Mississippi valley.

The Forty-Eighters

A small but very significant group of Germans left Europe for political reasons. The years between 1830 and 1848 were ones of political upheaval in Germany. The rulers of the small German states were trying to suppress the democratic ideas that had been spread by the French Revolution. But these ideas of self-government and economic freedom, once released, lived on. Just as in France almost half a century earlier, a growing number of people wanted representative systems of government and political equality for everyone. Others also wanted to see the German states united, so that Germany could become a power alongside other European countries.

Revolutions aimed at achieving these goals broke out in Germany in 1830 and 1848. Motivated by a successful revolution in France, groups of prosperous farmers, artisans, and skilled laborers attempted to overthrow the royal powers in order to gain a voice in their governments. But unlike the French king, the monarchies of Germany were successful in crushing the revolutions. Many who felt they could not live under the tyranny of the German ruling classes immigrated to the United States. Other dissidents, fearing revenge from the royal powers in Germany, fled for their lives.

The political refugees who came to the United States after the failed 1848 revolution were called the forty-

eighters. Among them were people of excellent training and education. For many years to come, they would
provide intellectual and political leadership in German-
American communities throughout the United States.

The forty-eighters were idealists who found much to
criticize. For some years, these Germans were very
outspoken in their judgment of the U.S. government
and tried to improve it. Some had plans to create a
separate German state in the United States. Their most
powerful spokespersons were often newspaper editors,
frequently of German-language newspapers such as the
St. Louis Anzeiger des Westerns; the Volksblatt in Cincinnati; the New York Staats Zeitung; and the Buffalo
Democrat.

As seen in this mural, many German immigrants journeyed over the Oregon Trail to settle in the West.

This criticism of the United States aroused unfriendly reactions from non–German Americans. The tensions contributed to the creation of a political party called the American Party, composed mainly of native-born Americans whose ancestors were mostly British. Members of the American Party were also known as "Know-Nothings." The Know-Nothings worked through secret societies to make sure that candidates sympathetic to their views were elected to public offices. When accused of using illegal methods to exert their influence, they claimed that they "knew nothing" about the secret societies, and that is how the party got its name.

Know-Nothings believed that immigrants were trying to bring the United States under the control of foreign powers. They were suspicious of all immigrants of the Roman Catholic faith (mostly the Irish), believ-

Left: This cartoon, published in 1872, warned people of the evils of the bigoted Know-Nothing Party. Right: Carl Schurz, one of the most famous forty-eighters.

ing that they would try to bring the United States under the power of the pope. They also mistrusted the German immigrants because many of the immigrants criticized the U.S. political system. Many immigrant groups, especially Germans and Irish, were subject to verbal and physical abuse and job discrimination.

Because of their suspicion of foreigners, the Know-Nothings favored limiting government office to native-born American citizens. They also wanted to impose a 21-year wait for immigrants who wished to become citizens. Know-Nothings sought to limit the sale of liquor and to have the Protestant Bible read daily in public school classrooms. But the Know-Nothings were never very popular. Their peak came when they backed former president Millard Fillmore in his 1856 bid for reelection. Although the Know-Nothings won more than 21 percent of the popular vote and eight electoral votes, the Democrat James Buchanan won the election.

The differences between the forty-eighters and the more established German Americans resulted in tensions between the two groups. Not everyone wanted sweeping reforms of the government or a separate German state in the United States. Opposing groups debated the issues in German-language newspapers.

The German intellectuals who came to the United States, like all other immigrants, first worked at whatever jobs they could find. They farmed, dug canals, and heaved picks to build railroads. But many of them were well educated and felt as though they were wasting their abilities. It was not unusual to hear them recite Latin and Greek as they worked. This practice resulted in the nickname "Latin farmers." Eventually, however, most of them found places in the professions for which they had been trained. They worked as doctors, teachers, engineers, and in other professional positions.

A forty-eighter named Carl Schurz became one of the most famous German immigrants in the history of the United States. Because of involvement in the failed revolution in Germany in 1848, he was forced to abandon his career as a history professor. He came to the United States in 1852, a young man in his mid-twenties.

Schurz settled on a farm near Watertown, Wisconsin. Wisconsin, Minnesota, and Missouri were three states where the forty-eighters hoped to set up a "New Germany." But Schurz had little patience with the idea of a German state within a state. He felt that the future of German immigrants was completely tied to the future of the United States, not to a separate German country. He quickly learned English and became a patriotic citizen. An ardent opponent of slavery, Schurz soon was active in the new Republican Party. He became a friend of Abraham Lincoln, for whom he campaigned hard in 1860, the year Lincoln was elected president. Schurz's influence with German-speaking voters was of great help. President Lincoln appointed Schurz United States minister to Spain in 1861, but he came home in 1862 to enlist in the Union army. During the Civil War, he distinguished himself in several battles, including the Battle of Gettysburg. By the end of the war, he had risen to the rank of major general.

A New Kind of Immigrant

Because most of the immigrants during this era continued to be skilled laborers, they settled in cities, where there were many job opportunities. German immigrants helped build some of the United States' leading cities—cities that still have large German-American populations: Rochester and Buffalo, New York; Cincinnati and Cleveland, Ohio; St. Louis, Missouri; and Milwaukee, Wisconsin. Many industries rapidly expanded during the second half of the century, and craftspeople and skilled laborers were in great demand.

German skilled laborers helped industrial expansion in the United States because they had been well trained under the traditional European system of apprenticeship. Under this system, workers and artisans of the same occupation formed a group known as a guild. Members of guilds established rules to control the quality of their product, such as cloth, glassware, or tex-

German settlers developed the Kentucky rifle, which was a more accurate weapon on the frontier than old-fashioned European rifles. German immigrants also created the Conestoga wagon. Popularly known as covered wagons, Conestogas carried thousands of immigrants across the frontier, and became a part of the legends of the Old West.

tiles. The immigrants brought the guild system with them to North America. Later, the guilds evolved into trade unions—organizations formed to ensure that workers were guaranteed certain rights and wages.

Trade unions became common in industrial cities during the 1830s. In the 1850s, German immigrants helped small unions unite into larger ones, strengthening their bargaining power and helping workers obtain better hours and improved working conditions.

Most of the Germans who came to the United States in the 19th century came to improve themselves economically. Thousands were farmers attracted by the cheap, fertile land that could be had for two or three dollars an acre in the newly opened areas of the American West. In 1862 Congress passed the Homestead Act, making land practically free. One hundred sixty acres were available to anyone who was at least 21 years old and agreed to live on the land for a minimum of five years, to make improvements on the property, and to pay modest fees. Some groups of immigrants sent agents ahead of them to select the best farming areas.

By 1860 Germans accounted for nearly one-third of the total number of foreign-born residents in the United States. Between 1845 and 1861 alone, 1,250,000 German immigrants landed in the United States. In part, the flood of immigration was accelerated by improvements in ocean transportation. By the 1850s, steamships generally had replaced sailing vessels. Steam-driven ships reduced the transatlantic voyage from six weeks to two. They also made cheaper fares possible. In the United States, steamboats also made it easier for immigrants to move within the country—along rivers such as the Ohio and the Mississippi. By 1860 several railroads linked the major cities of the east coast with the Mississippi River, and it was along these railroad lines that the immigrant trains passed. By 1869 a traveler could cross the entire country by rail. Immigrants could move farther, faster, and cheaper than ever before.

German Americans found work in flour mills, such as this one in New Ulm, Minnesota.

German Americans soon lived in all areas of the country and took part in the major events of the 19th century. Some went to Texas when it was an independent republic (called the Lone Star Republic). Many then became U.S. citizens after Texas became part of the United States in 1845. Other Germans followed the trails westward and participated in the California gold rush or made the long trek to Oregon.

Groups of Germans also moved west together and formed towns in places such as Texas, Colorado, and Minnesota. New Ulm, Minnesota, was one of the "little Germanys" founded all across the East and Midwest. Newly arriving immigrants could expect to find familiar surroundings in New Ulm. German shops, theaters, churches, schools, and social clubs all helped to ease the shock of moving to a vast new country. Many of these communities, including New Ulm, still retain their German heritage.

The Civil War

The Civil War officially began in 1861 after the fall of Fort Sumter. Eleven Southern states had seceded from the Union over the issue of slavery to form the Confederate States of America. President Lincoln was determined to keep the country together. Upon President Lincoln's first call for volunteers, an estimated 4,000 Germans in Pennsylvania and New York enlisted.

But German Americans fought in both the Union and Confederate armies. One historian estimates that 176,817 Union soldiers had been born in Germany. Other estimates are as high as 300,000. Entire regiments were formed of German volunteers. Many of the men could not speak English and received commands in German.

Despite the large turnout of German Americans, there were conflicting feelings within the German community about the war. On one hand, the forty-eighters, who helped lead the Germans of the Union into the war,

German Americans pose for family portraits in the mid-1800s.

fought to end slavery. They opposed many of their fellow midwesterners, who were not really concerned with the abolition of slavery or the preservation of the Union. On the other hand, the German sectarians in the North held on to their pacifist beliefs and were excused from combat as conscientious objectors. Some of these people made financial contributions to support the war. Others worked in noncombat roles, as teamsters (driving teams of horses) or hospital orderlies.

In Missouri, German Americans were also at odds with their non-German neighbors over the war. The governor of the state was opposed to Lincoln and his antislavery policies. But the Germans living in and around St. Louis, Missouri, raised an artillery regiment and four infantry regiments for Lincoln. The German-born forces were so successful on the battlefield that, despite their governor, they defeated Confederate forces at Camp Jackson and brought Missouri to the side of the Union.

German-American farmers in Nebraska, mid-1800s

The Civil War also raised some anti-German senti-ment. The large number of foreign-born soldiers, espe-cially Germans, aroused some hostility. This was a carryover of the hostility to immigrants that had been the focus of the Know-Nothings. While German troops fought valiantly and successfully at such important bat-tles as Bull Run and Shiloh, defeats at Chancellorsville and Gettysburg provoked a debate over the worth of the German troops.

The army of the Confederacy had German troops, too. Nicola Marschall, who had been born in Prussia, designed the Confederate uniform and flag. Karl Ustav Memminger, born in Württemburg, was the Confed-eracy's secretary of the treasury. There was little anti-German sentiment in the South—probably because the German settlers were not recent immigrants.

The end of the Civil War brought another immense wave of emigration from Germany, larger than any previous wave. Germans began to emigrate by the tens and hundreds of thousands in 1870, the year the Franco-Prussian War began in Europe. German citizens fled to avoid war, conscription (forced military service), and the harshness of the Prussian drive to unite the small German states into one country. By 1900 nearly 2,700,000 Germans who had been born in Europe were living in the United States.

After the War

In the last years of the 19th century, German immigra-tion changed. More skilled laborers and industrial workers than farmers entered the country. These laborers did not choose to leave Germany for the same reasons as the farmers who had gone to the United States before them. Bad weather and poverty had driven farmers away from Germany early on. Only after the revolutions in Europe and the resulting political upheavals in Germany did life become hard for larger numbers of skilled laborers and industrial workers. They too struck out for a better life in the United States.

In 1884 the growing federation of national trade unions—created in large part by German immigrants—demanded an eight-hour working day by May 1, 1886. Despite newspaper claims that unionists were "mostly Communists...[and] nearly all foreigners," by May 1, 20,000 workers in Chicago had won their eight-hour day.

A demonstration was held on May 3, 1886, at the McCormick Harvester Plant in Chicago, where a strike was in progress. Police hostile to the demonstrators intervened and one striker was killed and several were hurt. The next evening, unionists called a meeting to protest these events.

Though as many as 25,000 were expected, only 3,000 people showed up, and many left as rain began to fall. A *Chicago Tribune* reporter described the meeting as "peaceable and quiet." Nonetheless, the anti-labor Captain "Black Jack" Bonfield of the Chicago police formed his officers into ranks and marched into the meeting. A bomb was thrown by angry unionists, which in turn resulted in traded gunfire between police and union demonstrators. Seven police officers were killed and more than sixty people were wounded. Police arrested every suspected unionist they found. The incident came to be called the Haymarket Riot.

Thirty-one of those arrested were brought to trial, charged with participating in planning a lethal bomb blast that killed policeman Mathias J. Degan. One of the German Americans charged, Louis Lingg, was a known bomb maker. On the other hand, the evidence against another of those German Americans indicted, Oscar Neebe, "would not justify a five dollar fine," according to one witness.

Neebe was sentenced to 15 years in prison. Seven others, including Lingg, were sentenced to hang. All of them were executed, except for Lingg, who killed himself in his cell with a bomb he managed to construct there.

Although the Haymarket Riot and other incidents of union-related violence increased some anti-immigrant—and especially anti-German—feeling in the United States, not all German Americans were involved in the

unions. Many of them were farmers and established peaceful relations with their neighbors.

The Haymarket Riot in Chicago, 1886

According to the U.S. census of 1900, the great majority of farmers in the United States were German immigrants. These figures show that there were 522,252 farmers who were either German-born or descended from earlier German immigrants, compared with 183,157 farmers of Anglo-Saxon origin and 174,694 farmers from Scandinavian countries. Yet even as German Americans became more settled into American life, a conflict was brewing back in Europe that would threaten to break the bonds that the immigrants tried to build.

3
WORLD WAR I
AND THE 20th CENTURY

World War I (known as the Great War) began suddenly as a result of the assassination of the heir to the throne of Austria-Hungary, Archduke Francis Ferdinand, on June 28, 1914. The archduke was killed by a Bosnian who was upset with the Austro-Hungarian Empire's treatment of his country. While this violent event set off the first major war of the 20th century, the causes of the war went back much further.

Throughout the late 19th and early 20th centuries, the nations of Europe were increasingly at odds with each other over their various colonies. Rivalries among France, Russia, Britain, and Germany over holdings in Africa, Asia, and the Balkans (a group of countries in southeastern Europe) increased tensions in Europe.

The industrialization of Europe allowed for the manufacture of high-powered weapons. Guns and cannons were more sophisticated. Ships were built of iron instead of wood. Machine guns, hand grenades, and land mines were also newly available to armies.

Industrialization also led to enormous population increases all over Europe. The use of machinery in manufacturing and agriculture allowed the economies of the European countries to grow substantially. This new wealth made it possible for some people to afford healthier lifestyles and to support larger families. The growing populations made it possible to raise much larger armies and navies.

Germany, which had unified in 1871 under the leadership of Otto von Bismarck, was anxious to demonstrate its power as one of the great nations of Europe. Germans wanted to increase their colonial empire and build a navy. Tension created by the competition for foreign colonies added to the disharmony among Germany, France, and Britain.

Finally, the primary cause of World War I was the alliance system. The empire of Austria-Hungary was allied with Germany—an alliance known as the Central Powers. Britain, France, and Russia were in an alliance called the Triple Entente. After Archduke Ferdinand of Austria was assassinated in Serbia, Austria-Hungary declared war on Serbia. The Germans went to war alongside their ally, Austria-Hungary,

A German family receives identification tags at Ellis Island before a railroad trip, 1905.

43

and soon the Central Powers were fighting the Triple Entente—World War I had begun.

The outbreak of the war was the beginning of a great crisis for the German-American community. Eleven percent of all U.S. citizens had at least one German-born parent. More than one-third of these people were born in Germany themselves.

During the first three years of the war, Germany fought with Britain, France, and their allies. The United States remained neutral, supporting neither side. At first, German Americans were largely supporters of Germany's cause. Most of this support was found among the Germans who had immigrated to the United States after the Civil War. They had not completely lost their attachment to Germany, as had many earlier German immigrants.

Feelings of German nationalism were encouraged by hundreds of German-language newspapers. By the beginning of the 20th century, German Americans who could speak and write German well were growing older and retiring, and the young writers who took their places spoke English. Editors of German-language newspapers began to import writers from Germany itself. These people gave an entirely new tone to the German-American press, and their writing was often more concerned with admiring accounts of events in Germany than with what was going on in the United States.

When the United States finally allied itself with Britain and France and declared war on Germany in 1917, many non-German Americans reacted with strong anti-German sentiment. The study of the German language was dropped from public schools. Hundreds of German newspapers stopped publishing. German music was eliminated from opera and orchestral programs. German singing societies were disbanded. All things German were suspect, with sometimes ridiculous results. Sauerkraut was given the new name "liberty cabbage," and dachshunds were renamed "liberty hounds." Even the hamburger was called a "salisbury steak" for a while.

44

During the wave of anti-German feeling, many German-American families, some of whom had been in the United States for generations, changed their names. Businesses that made use of the word "German" changed it to something else. "German-American" banks, for example, became "North American" banks.

Yet the widespread anti-German sentiment and highly vocal criticism of everything German caused many German Americans to be much more pro-German than they might have been otherwise. They were infuriated that the anti-German slur "Hun" was applied to them and their relatives, both in the United States and in Europe. Even President Woodrow Wilson denounced what he called "hyphenated Americans," calling into question the loyalty of those who claimed connections to both the United States and Germany.

Anti-German feelings stirred up by World War I led to the removal of the mythic goddess Germania from an insurance building in St. Paul, Minnesota and to the burning of the German Kaiser in effigy in New York City.

45

World War I ended with Germany's surrender. A treaty, signed in Versailles, France, on June 28, 1919, limited the amount of troops and armaments that Germany could maintain. It also required Germany to pay for damages that the victors had suffered during the war.

For the German-American community, World War I accelerated the pace of assimilation. Forced by anti-German attitudes to abandon the German language and change German names, German Americans became less German and more American as the century progressed.

Despite the wave of anti-German sentiment during World War I, many German-American families remained proudly patriotic, like this St. Paul, Minnesota, family posing in front of their home.

German Immigration in the 20th Century

The first 10 years of the 20th century saw a decline in German immigration. Although the number of immigrants in this period totaled 341,498 and was still large compared to the number coming from other countries, it was the smallest number of Germans to come to the United States in 70 years. During the next 10 years, which was the period of World War I, the number of German immigrants fell to the lowest level since the 1830s.

Immigration picked up again after the war. The defeat of Germany brought severe inflation, unemployment, and economic depression to that nation. German immigration to the United States in the 1920s increased to almost three times more than the previous ten years.

As immigration changed in the 20th century, so did the nature of German-American life. A combination of anti-German sentiment and assimilation meant that traces of German culture in the United States continued to fade. The German bands that played on the street corners were gone, as were German butchers, beer gardens, summer-night festivals, and May wine parades.

World War II

The peace in Europe was to be short-lived. In the early 1920s, it became apparent that Germany could not afford to make the payments, called reparations, to the victorious nations of World War I. Economic depression, which began in the United States in 1929, soon spread to Europe. Still struggling with its losses from the war, Germany was hardest hit. In the turmoil, Adolf Hitler came to power on January 30, 1933.

Hitler, a former housepainter and failed army corporal, rejected violently any suggestion that Germany be held to the Treaty of Versailles. He believed that Germany should expand its borders to include all German peoples in other nations of Europe. He also believed that a group of white people he called "Aryans" were a "master race," entitled to dominate the world. He declared himself "the führer," or leader, of Germany.

He rejected such ideas as equality under law and majority rule, saying the government had the right to achieve its ends by any means necessary. To this end, he announced in October 1933 that Germany would begin to rearm itself without regard to the limits imposed by the Treaty of Versailles. Two years later he reinstated mandatory military service for all German males. The military buildup had begun again.

With Hitler's rise to power, German immigration to the United States declined, but the immigration that did occur took on a new character. Hitler's ideas of Aryan racial superiority brought widespread political and religious persecution in Germany. The main targets of this persecution were the German Jews, but they were not alone. Hitler's political party, the Nazis, persecuted their opponents, including Protestant and Catholic religious leaders who protested Hitler's policies; leaders of other political parties; independent thinkers; university professors; and trade unionists. Many of these people fled Germany to save their lives, and the United

Before the United States entered World War II, nearly 20,000 Americans—many of them of German descent—joined the pro-Nazi Bund. The Bund was led by Fritz Kuhn, an American citizen.

States received a new wave of immigrants much like the forty-eighters—scientists, businesspeople, writers, and scholars. Many of these refugees were Jewish.

In March 1938, Hitler forcibly annexed Austria to Germany. One year later, the German army occupied Czechoslovakia. But it wasn't until Germany invaded Poland on September 1, 1939, that Britain and France declared war and World War II officially began.

As in World War I, the United States was at first neutral. Feeling injured by the heavy casualties of the last war in Europe, the United States did not want to get involved in another destructive war. Yet an attack at Pearl Harbor, Hawaii, by Germany's ally Japan in December 1941 forced the United States to join the Allies—Britain and France—and enter the conflict.

German Americans and World War II

During World War II, there was little of the anti-German hysteria that swept the United States during World War I. Nor was there much pro-Nazi feeling on the part of the great majority of German Americans. One pro-Nazi German-American organization did exist, however, in the 1930s. This was the German-American Bund, led by Fritz Kuhn, a former chemical engineer who was sometimes called "the American Führer."

Headquarters of the Bund was in Yorkville, a section of New York City with a large German population. The core members of the Bund were German Americans who admired Hitler and his programs. Hundreds of members were not German, but they shared the Bund's admiration for the German dictator. Kuhn and his "storm troopers" claimed a membership of 200,000, but one expert placed the number closer to 20,000. During the late 1930s, members of the Bund held rallies, made speeches, dressed in jackboots and Nazi insignias, and marched carrying the Nazi swastika flag to emulate Hitler's German army. When the United States entered World War II, and Hitler and the Nazi Party became the United States' official enemies, the Bund collapsed.

During World War II, approximately one-third of the 15 million men and women who served in the U.S. armed forces were of German or part-German ancestry. General Dwight D. Eisenhower, who became the supreme commander of the Allies in Europe, was the descendant of a family of German sectarians who settled in Pennsylvania in 1732. Like most sectarians, the Eisenhowers were pacifists and General Eisenhower's choice of the army as a career was a departure from the early traditions of his family.

Postwar Germany

After World War II ended with an Allied victory in 1945, Germany was divided and occupied by the four Allies. British, French, and U.S. forces advancing from the west met the Soviet armies marching in from the east. After the occupation, the western half of Germany was called the Federal Republic of Germany, or West Germany.

German Americans all over the country celebrate their heritage at festivals such as Oktoberfest and Steuben Day parades.

West Germany, in the tradition of France, Great Britain, and the United States, had a democratic government and became the ally of these countries. East Germany—also known as the German Democratic Republic—adopted a government set up by the Soviet Union and became allied with that country. The former capital city of Berlin, located entirely inside of East Germany, was also physically split in half. West Berlin remained democratic, while East Berlin became the capital of East Germany.

Those opposing viewpoints between the socialist countries of the east and the democratic republics of the west became more pronounced in the late 1940s and 1950s in what was later called the Cold War. The Cold War was marked by mutual distrust and an escalating arms race between the two sides.

The Cold War lasted about 40 years until the rise to power of Mikhail Gorbachev in the Soviet Union. While Gorbachev attempted to bring greater freedoms to his country, the influence of the Soviet Union in East Germany waned, until in late 1989 the socialist government was overthrown in a peaceful revolution. On October 3, 1990, East and West Germany were reunited into a single country called Germany for the first time since the end of World War II.

4
CONTRIBUTIONS TO AMERICAN LIFE

Business and Industry

One of U.S. history's most famous self-made entrepreneurs, John Jacob Astor, emigrated from Germany in 1783 when he was 20 years old. His father was a butcher and John had little schooling. During his voyage to the United States, however, he met a fur trader, and by the time Astor had landed he had chosen a career.

For a time, he traded in furs and sold musical instruments. He had brought seven flutes with him to the United States. By 1800 Astor had amassed a fortune of about a quarter of a million dollars. In 1808 he organized the American Fur Company. By the late 1820s, the American Fur Company had become the leading trader in the Great Lakes and Rocky Mountain areas.

Astor sold out in 1834 when he decided the fur trade was a dying business. After withdrawing from the fur trade, Astor went to New York City, where he continued to invest in real estate and other ventures. He also built New York's Astor House, the first in a series of Astor family hotels.

At the time of his death in 1848, he was said to have been worth $20,000,000—the richest person in the country. In his will, he left the public libraries of New York vast sums of money.

John Jacob Bausch and Henry Lomb, two German immigrants, started a company in Rochester, New York, in 1849, that became internationally famous for its optical goods. Bausch was a skilled optician and Lomb a business executive. The company went through many trying years, because of a common prejudice that American-made lenses were inferior to those made in Europe. Nevertheless, by 1908 Bausch and Lomb was the largest lens manufacturer in the world, producing more than 20 million lenses annually for eyeglasses, cameras, microscopes, binoculars, and projectors.

John Jacob Bausch (left) and Henry Lomb

John Augustus Roebling, who became famous as a bridge builder, was also a German immigrant. After graduating from the Royal Polytechnic Institute in Berlin, he moved to Pennsylvania. While working as a canal engineer, Roebling developed a new kind of towrope that was made of steel cable instead of hemp. In 1846 he completed the first suspension bridge at Pittsburgh, Pennsylvania. His greatest accomplishment was the construction of a suspension bridge at Niagara Falls, New York. This giant structure was 821 feet long, and for nearly 50 years it held up under the strain of heavy train traffic. Roebling died while his famous Brooklyn Bridge was under construction. His son, Washington Augustus Roebling, who was also an engineer, completed it.

A Studebaker parade in Deadwood, South Dakota

During the California gold rush, a German immigrant named Levi Strauss made his fortune—in pants, not gold. Strauss, born in Bavaria in 1829, arrived in the United States when he was 14. In the early 1850s, he went to San Francisco to find gold and instead invented what continues to be a very popular article of clothing—denim blue jeans. Since then, more than one billion pairs of "Levi's" have been sold worldwide.

Henry Engelhard Steinweg began making pianos in the kitchen of his house in a tiny mountain town in Germany. Then he moved to the United States, modified his name to Steinway, and soon he and his sons were putting together pianos in a loft in New York City. His daughter sold them as fast as they were finished by offering free piano lessons to prospective customers. The firm that came to be known as Steinway & Sons was born.

The Studebaker brothers, Henry and Clement, opened a wagon building and blacksmith's shop in 1852 in South Bend, Indiana, with an initial investment of $68. During the Civil War, the Studebakers produced chuck wagons, ambulances, and artillery equipment for the Union army. By 1895 they were the world's largest wagon producers, turning out 75,000 horse-drawn vehicles every year. Then came the automobile. In 1919, having manufactured gun carriages, artillery wheels, escort wagons, tank wagons, and ambulances for the army during World War I, the company discontinued all wagon production to concentrate on cars. Today the Studebaker Corporation is a large diversified manufacturing company, but is no longer in the automobile business.

German names dominated the early years of the brewing industry and still do, with companies such as Pabst, Anheuser-Busch, Schlitz, Schmidt, Hamm, Pfeiffer, and Blatz. In the food industry, the companies with the names Heinz, Hershey, Kraft, and Fleischmann were all founded by German immigrants, to mention just a few.

Henry J. Heinz, who was born in Pittsburgh, Pennsylvania, in 1844, was descended from German im-

The Brooklyn Bridge

55

migrants. While working in his father's brickyard, he began marketing garden surplus. When he was only 16, he had his own hotbeds and was raising and distributing vegetables. While in his twenties, he began manufacturing pickles, spices, relishes, and other prepared foods. The slogan "57 varieties" was originated by Heinz in 1896. Actually, his company made more than 57 products, but he liked the sound of the number 57 and believed it was his lucky number. By the time of his death in 1919, the H. J. Heinz Company employed more than 6,000 people and had 25 branch offices.

H. J. Heinz (in wagon) liked to personally visit his workers, urging them on to greater productivity.

Benjamin Altman and Nathan Straus were two prominent merchants of German and Jewish descent. Altman founded a famous New York department store, and Straus, who was born in Otterberg, Germany, developed Macy's in New York, one of the best-known department stores in the United States. John Wanamaker was another merchant of German ancestry. He founded the large Philadelphia department store that bears his name.

The Rockefeller family is descended from Johann Peter Rockefeller, who came to the United States from the Rhineland in Germany in the early 1720s. One historian, however, says that John D. Rockefeller, who was born in 1839 and founded the Standard Oil Company and the family fortune, was "three-sixteenths or less" German, showing the extent of ethnic and racial mixing and blending in the United States by the late 1800s.

The Wanamaker department store in Philadelphia, 1885

Education

The Germans who came to the United States made some significant contributions to the nation's educational system. Margarethe Meyer Schurz, the wife of Carl Schurz, was a pioneer in children's education. She organized the first kindergarten in the United States at Watertown, Wisconsin, in the 1850s. By 1873 kindergartens were popular enough to cause the St. Louis, Missouri, school board to establish a public kindergarten system. Nearly all of the first kindergarten teachers were German immigrants.

Margarethe Schurz

Another German contribution to American education was the addition of physical education programs. The inspiration for physical training came mainly from the German Turner Societies, first organized in Germany during the early 19th century. The founders of the Turner Societies hoped that by stressing physical education and strength, German patriotism would also be strengthened. As these societies grew, they emphasized both physical and mental improvement.

The first American Turner Societies were organized in 1848, and the American Turners dedicated their first building two years later in Cincinnati, Ohio. Within a few years, the United States had 60 Turner Societies, all led by instructors who had received their physical education in Germany. Largely because of the Turners, physical education was added to many public school curricula, and some schools started gymnastic programs. In 1875 the Turners founded a school in Milwaukee for the purpose of training physical education instructors.

Science and Medicine

Among the German immigrants of the 19th and 20th centuries were many doctors. They had fine reputations and were leaders in improving medical training and practice. In an era when general practice was the rule, some of the German doctors were skilled specialists. Dr. Abraham Jacobi, for example, was a famous pediatrician and authority on children's diseases and infant feeding. He opened the United States' first free clinic for treatment of children's diseases and published eight volumes on medicine. Dr. Simon Baruch, who had been an assistant surgeon for the Confederate army, improved surgery methods, particularly for appendicitis. He was the father of Bernard Baruch, financier and statesperson.

The famous German-American scientist and inventor Charles Proteus Steinmetz was born in Breslau, Germany, in 1865. The genius behind the development of the General Electric Corporation, Steinmetz came to the United States in 1889. He had to flee Germany because of a provocative editorial he wrote for a socialist newspaper. Steinmetz is credited with more than 100 inventions necessary in the use of electricity. His most dramatic experiment was made in 1921 when

The Turner Society of New Ulm, Minnesota, 1885

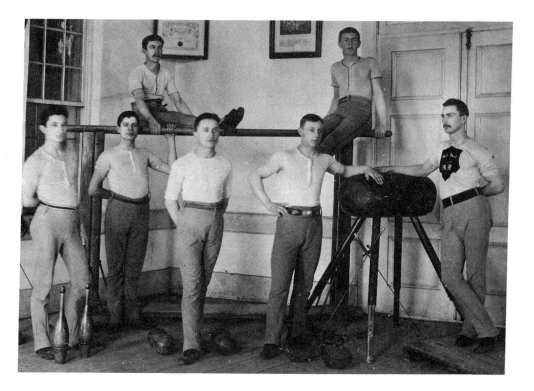

he created human-made lightning in his laboratory, so he could learn how to protect electrical systems from lightning damage.

One of the most famous of the refugees and exiles from Nazi Germany was Albert Einstein, a physicist and German Jew, who is regarded as one of the greatest minds of all time. He was born in 1879 at Ulm, Germany. When he was 15, he went to Switzerland, graduated from the University of Zurich, and became a Swiss citizen. He returned to Germany in 1913 as the director of the Kaiser Wilhelm Institute in Berlin and there, two years later, announced his famous theory of relativity. He was awarded the Nobel Prize in physics in 1921.

Albert Einstein

Einstein regained his German citizenship, but in 1933, while he was on a lecture tour of England and the United States, Hitler revoked it, stripped him of his position, and confiscated his property. Einstein moved to the United States and became director of the school of mathematics at the Institute for Advanced Study at Princeton, New Jersey. He became a U.S. citizen in 1940. He died in 1955.

J. Robert Oppenheimer was a descendant of German immigrants who was born in New York City in 1904. The son of a wealthy textile importer, Oppenheimer graduated from Harvard in 1925. He then studied in Göttingen, Germany, where he received a Ph.D. in physics. In 1929 he returned to the United States, where he studied physics at various universities until World War II. In 1943 he supervised the Los Alamos, New Mexico, laboratory where the atomic bomb was invented. He received the Medal of Merit from President Harry S. Truman in 1946 in recognition of his work. Oppenheimer died in 1967.

Government and Politics

Carl Schurz is probably one of the most famous German-American political activists. After the Civil War, Schurz made his home in St. Louis, Missouri, where he edited a German-language newspaper. In 1869 he was elected to be a U.S. senator from the state of Missouri. In 1877 he was named secretary of the interior by President Rutherford B. Hayes. In this position, Schurz championed a humane policy regarding the treatment of Native Americans and advocated preservation of public lands. After 1881 his career was mainly journalistic. He was an editor of the *New York Evening Post* and *Harper's Weekly*.

The first person of German descent to be elected president of the United States was Herbert Hoover in 1928. He was born in West Branch, Iowa, in 1874, and he made a large fortune as a mining engineer. In the years following World War I, Hoover headed the American Relief Administration and received world fame for his efforts to help the suffering people of Europe. The Republican convention of 1928 nominated him on the first ballot as the party's candidate for president. Hoover was not only the first person of German ancestry but also the first Quaker to be elected president.

The second U.S. president of German descent was Dwight D. Eisenhower. He was born in Texas in 1890 and raised in Abilene, Kansas. After graduating from the United States Military Academy at West Point in 1915, he followed a military career that led to the position of supreme commander of the Allied forces in Europe during World War II.

Following World War II, Eisenhower was army chief of staff. Upon his retirement, he was appointed president of Columbia University. In 1952 Eisenhower was elected the 34th president of the United States, the first Republican president in 20 years. He served two terms in office, from 1952 to 1960. During his administration, the Korean War ended, the United States launched its first satellite into orbit around the planet, and Alaska and Hawaii were admitted into the Union. When his presidency ended, Eisenhower made a now-famous speech warning of the buildup of the military, which indeed expanded at a rapid rate until the end of the Cold War. Eisenhower died in 1969.

Another distinguished German American in the field of political affairs is Henry Kissinger. Born in Furth, Ger-

A 1952 campaign button for Dwight D. Eisenhower

many, in 1923, Kissinger was 15 years old when he and his parents came to the United States to escape Nazi persecution. He was educated at Harvard University, where he later became a professor of international relations. In 1969 he joined the Nixon administration as a top-level advisor. He conducted important negotiations with foreign leaders and took part in drawing up the peace agreement that took U.S. troops out of the Vietnam War. In 1973 Kissinger won the Nobel Peace Prize. That same year, President Nixon appointed him secretary of state—a position Kissinger held until 1977. As secretary of state, Henry Kissinger continued his diplomatic efforts, most notably as a mediator in an Arab-Israeli conflict. In 1983 he was appointed chairperson of the bipartisan commission on Central America.

Henry Kissinger with Indian prime minister Indira Gandhi

Entertainment

German names in the entertainment world include film director Ernst Lubitsch; actor-director Erich von Stroheim, who is remembered particularly for his roles as Nazi officers; and film star Marlene Dietrich. Theatrical producer Florenz Ziegfeld was famed for his "Ziegfeld Follies," musical revues that highlighted a chorus line of beautiful dancers in lavish costume. The Ziegfeld Follies influenced American fashion in the 1920s.

Film actor Grace Kelly, whose mother was of German descent, was born in Philadelphia, Pennsylvania, in 1929. She was educated at the American Academy of Dramatic Arts in New York City, from which she graduated in 1949. She acted on stage on and off Broadway until her film debut in 1951. In the next five years, Kelly made several films: *Dial M for Murder, High Society, Rear Window,* and *The Country Girl,* for which she won an Academy Award. In 1956 she married Prince Rainier of Monaco, a small nation near southern France, and she became the Princess of Monaco. She died there in 1982.

Marlene Dietrich

One of the great names of the Broadway theater in the 20th century was Lotte Lenya. Born to a poor German coach driver and his wife in 1898, she moved to Zurich in 1913 to begin a career as a dancer and actor. There she adopted the name Lotte Lenya. Seven years later, she moved to Berlin, where she met her first husband, Kurt Weill.

Weill was a noted lyricist and playwright who worked on such famous plays as *The Threepenny Opera*, *Mahagonny*, and *The Seven Deadly Sins*. The couple fled Nazi Germany for the United States in the 1930s. Weill's career soared in the 1930s and 1940s, while Lenya's took longer to build. Lenya's greatest successes

Grace Kelly

Lotte Lenya (right) in the James Bond movie From Russia with Love

came after her husband's early death in 1950. She is most noted for her performances in 1954's *The Threepenny Opera* and *Cabaret* in 1966. She also appeared in several films, including a 1964 James Bond movie called *From Russia With Love.* Lenya died in 1981.

One of the great legacies to entertainment in the United States was left by a German-American family of the 19th century. Alfred, Albert, Otto, Charles, and John Ringling were born in the 1850s and 1860s in the American Midwest. The brothers developed a show that included skits, clown acts, animal acts, and a band. They began to tour the country. In 1888 they bought their first elephant, and two years later the Ringling Brothers Circus was the biggest rival to Barnum and Bailey.

The Ringling Brothers Circus continued to grow and in 1907 bought the Barnum and Bailey organization. By 1930 Ringling Brothers Barnum and Bailey was the largest circus in the world, employing 5,000 people. The main tent seated 10,000 people. Two hundred forty-nine railroad cars were needed to transport employees, performers, animals, and equipment. The organization stopped expanding in 1930 because of economic depression and competition from other forms of entertainment. The last of the brothers, "Mr. John," died in 1936. The circus was owned and run by the Ringling family until it was sold in 1967. It still bears the Ringling name.

One immigrant who moved to the United States as a result of World War II is film director Billy Wilder. Born in 1906, Wilder is known for films that are of consistently high quality and diversity. *The Major and the Minor* (1942) was a farce that demonstrated to Hollywood Wilder's comic abilities. In 1945 Wilder's *The Lost Weekend* won an Academy Award. Wilder is also known for popular comedies such as *Some Like It Hot* (1959) and *The Apartment* (1960).

Rod Steiger was born in Westhampton, New York, in 1925. At the age of 26, he began a distinguished acting career. His most notable roles have been in *On the Waterfront* (1954), *The Pawnbroker* (1964), and *In the Heat of the Night* (1967), for which he won an Academy Award.

Sports

There are many German names in the field of sports, including baseball players Babe Ruth, Honus Wagner, Heinie Manush, and Lou Gehrig. Some of the greatest American swimmers have been of German ancestry. Among them is Johnny Weissmuller, who was also the movies' best-known and most popular "Tarzan."

Daughter of a New Jersey butcher born in Württemberg and a mother born in East Prussia, Gertrude Ederle was born in 1906. By age 19, she held 29 amateur national and world swimming records. As a member of the 1924 U.S. Olympic team, she helped win the gold medal in the 400-meter freestyle relay. On August 6, 1926, Ederle became the first woman to swim the English Channel.

Detlef Schrempf, a professional basketball player for the Seattle Supersonics, was born in Leverkusen, West Germany, in 1963, but grew up in the United States. He was named to the 1993 NBA All-Star team.

Johnny Weissmuller

Babe Ruth (left) and Lou Gehrig

Detlef Schrempf (left)

Music and Literature

The German passion for music has greatly enriched American culture. English colonists, particularly the Puritans, regarded music as frivolous and unnecessary. The Germans were pioneers in introducing both formal and folk music to their new country. The beginnings of America's great choral societies can be traced to German singing societies. These groups commonly entertained at public celebrations, such as Fourth of July parades. The Germans were also leaders in establishing chamber music ensembles and symphony orchestras.

In 1848, 23 German refugees in New York City founded the Germania Orchestra, one of the first symphony orchestras in the United States. They toured the country for six years, giving 800 concerts. They not only introduced the works of such composers as Beethoven and Wagner to U.S. audiences, but they also inspired others to form orchestras, too. Nearly all the members of the Germania Orchestra became conductors or concert leaders of new orchestras.

Leopold Damrosch, the violinist and conductor, founded the New York Symphony Society and the New York Oratorio Society. His son, Walter Johannes Damrosch, a conductor and composer, was widely known for popularizing music through the medium of radio broadcasts. John Philip Sousa, "the March King," and America's most famous composer of band music, was partly of German descent.

Literary figures of German descent include H. L. Mencken, John Gunther, Emil Ludwig, and Theodore Dreiser, to mention only a few. Dreiser began his writing career as a newspaper reporter and magazine editor in Chicago and New York. His concern for social justice helped him become one of America's first realistic novelists. Two of his outstanding works are *Sister Carrie* and *An American Tragedy*.

John Steinbeck, one of the most influential authors of the first half of the 20th century, was born in Salinas, California, in 1902 to a German father and Irish mother.

Steinbeck studied at Stanford University and worked at odd jobs until the publication of his little-noticed first novel, *Cup of Gold,* in 1929. During the Great Depression, Steinbeck lived among poor migrant workers in southern California. A novel about these people, 1937's *Of Mice and Men,* brought Steinbeck both fame and critical recognition. The high point of his writing career came with the publication in 1939 of *The Grapes of Wrath,* a novel about poor Oklahoma farmers driven from their land and their attempts to better their lives by resettling in California. The book was a best-seller for two years and won a National Book Award and Pulitzer Prize for fiction. In 1962 he won the Nobel Prize for literature. Steinbeck died in New York City in 1968.

Kurt Vonnegut was born in Indianapolis, Indiana, in 1922, the son of a German-American architect, Kurt Vonnegut Sr., and a German-American mother, Edith Lieber. During World War II, Vonnegut's U.S. Army division was sent to Europe. During the Battle of the Bulge in 1944, Vonnegut was captured and imprisoned in the city of Dresden, Germany. There he worked as a prisoner until the city was firebombed by Allied planes in February 1945. The bombardment, which resulted in an estimated 135,000 civilian deaths, became the subject of Vonnegut's first novel, *Slaughterhouse-Five,* published in 1969. Vonnegut has published novels, books of essays and speeches, plays, and screenplays.

Louise Erdrich

Another important author of the latter half of the 20th century is Louise Erdrich. Born in 1954 of German-American and Chippewa descent, Erdrich grew up in North Dakota. Her first novel, *Love Medicine* (1984), follows the lives of two Native American families in North Dakota. The book won both the Book Critics Circle Award and the *Los Angeles Times* award for the best novel of 1985. She followed that novel with two more in the series. The third of these, *Tracks,* brought Erdrich to best-seller status in 1988.

Two German Americans who, while not writers, have nonetheless contributed to American letters are cartoonists Thomas Nast and Charles Schulz. Thomas Nast originated two very familiar symbols, the Republican elephant and the Democratic donkey. Nast was born in Germany in 1840 and brought to New York by his mother when he was only six years old. As a child, he pursued his great love for drawing, and at 15 he was employed by Frank Leslie's *Illustrated Newspaper* to do sketches. The famous donkey and elephant were both well established in his pictures by 1874. Nast died in 1902.

Charles Monroe Schulz, born in 1922, is the creator of the famous *Peanuts* comic strip. After serving in World War II, he began to draw a comic strip for a St. Paul, Minnesota, newspaper. His rise to fame began in 1950, when *Peanuts* began to be distributed all across the United States. Within 20 years, it was one of the most widely distributed comic strips of all time. *Peanuts* has inspired television specials, a musical comedy called *You're a Good Man, Charlie Brown,* and a line of greeting cards. Schulz lives in California.

Charles Schulz

For more than 300 years, German Americans have had a wide range of influence on U.S. culture and history. Through hard work and determination, they have proven themselves to be a vital addition to the diverse country they now call home.

INDEX

ACKNOWLEDGMENTS: The photographs in this book are reproduced through the courtesy of: p. 2, The Cincinnati Historical Society; pp. 6–7, 9, 10–11, 22, 25, 41, 62 (top), Library of Congress; p. 12, Germantown Historical Society, Philadelphia, PA; p. 14, Kunsthistorische Museum; p. 15, The Henry Francis du Pont Winterthur Museum, Delaware; p. 16, Betty Groskin; p. 17, Charles S. Rice; p. 19, Lehigh County Historical Society; p. 21 (top and bottom), Salem County Historical Society, Salem, NJ; pp. 24–25, 32 (left), 48, 58 (top), 60, Independent Picture Service; p. 27, Lewis Miller: Sketches and Chronicles, York, PA; pp. 28–29, 45 (top), 46 (left), Minnesota Historical Society; p. 29, Albert Hummerich, Berlin; pp. 30–31, Oregon State Highway Department; p. 32 (right), U.S. Signal Corps, National Archives; pp. 35 (left), 61 (bottom), Smithsonian Institution; p. 35 (left), Oregon Historical Society; pp. 36, 37, 59, Brown County Historical Society; p. 38, Nebraska State Historical Society; p. 43, New York Public Library; p. 45 (bottom), Bettmann Archives; p. 65 (top right), National Archives; p. 50, Mark Ivins / Larimer Square; p. 53, Bausch & Lomb, Inc.; p. 54, Lori Olsen; p. 55, Stew Thornley; p. 56, H. J. Heinz Company; p. 57, Historical Society of Pennsylvania; p. 61 (top), U.S. Government Printing Office; p. 62 (bottom), CBS; p. 63 (top), TV Times; pp. 63 (bottom), 65 (bottom); p. 65 (top left), © Bruce Kluckhohn; p. 67, Michael Dorris; p. 68, Roddy McDowall.

Groups featured in Lerner's In America series:

AMERICAN INDIANS
CUBANS
DANES
FILIPINOS
FRENCH
GERMANS
GREEKS
IRISH
ITALIANS
JAPANESE

JEWS
KOREANS
LEBANESE
MEXICANS
NORWEGIANS
PUERTO RICANS
SCOTS &
   SCOTCH-IRISH
VIETNAMESE

Lerner Publications Company
241 First Avenue North • Minneapolis, Minnesota 55401